C000142866

Alexandra Harris is a literary
Educated at the University o
Institute, she worked for te
Liverpool, and is now Professo
of Birmingham. *Romantic Mo*
and the Imagination from Virgi
won the Guardian First Book Award and a Somerset
Maugham Award. *Weatherland: Writers and Artists Under
English Skies* (2015) was shortlisted for the Ondaatje
Prize and adapted for BBC Radio 4. Her latest book is
The Rising Down: Lives in a Sussex Landscape (2024).
A Fellow of the Royal Society of Literature, Harris
reviews for the *Guardian* and other publications
as well as judging literary prizes, writing for
exhibition catalogues and lecturing widely.

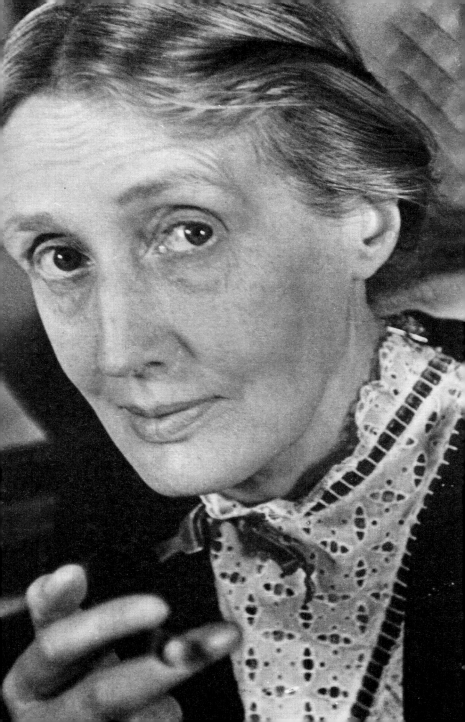

ALEXANDRA HARRIS

VIRGINIA WOOLF

with 46 illustrations

For my students in Liverpool
AH

COVER, IMAGE: Vanessa Bell, *Virginia Woolf, c.* 1912. Oil on panel, 41 × 31 cm (16.14 × 12.2 in.). National Trust Photographic Library. © Estate of Vanessa Bell. All rights reserved, DACS 2023/Bridgeman Images; PATTERN: Charleston Scumble pattern. Cambridge Imprint for the Charleston Trust, 2019. Courtesy Cambridge Imprint. FRONTISPIECE: Virginia Woolf by Gisèle Freund, June 1939.

First published in the United Kingdom in 2011 by
Thames & Hudson Ltd, 181A High Holborn,
London WC1V 7QX

First paperback edition published in 2013
This compact paperback edition published in 2024

Virginia Woolf © 2011, 2013 and 2024 Thames & Hudson
Ltd, London

Text © 2011 Alexandra Harris

Designed and typeset by Fred Birdsall studio

British Library Cataloguing-in-Publication Data
A catalogue record for this book is available from
the British Library

ISBN 978-0-500-29783-4

Printed and bound in the UK by CPI Group (UK) Ltd

MIX
Paper | Supporting
responsible forestry
FSC www.fsc.org   FSC® C171272

Be the first to know about our new releases,
exclusive content and author events by visiting
thamesandhudson.com
thamesandhudsonusa.com
thamesandhudson.com.au

Contents

Foreword

In 1907 Virginia Stephen was twenty-five and not yet a published novelist. Each week's living and each new piece of writing had a make-or-break quality to it. She did not know whether she would marry and have a family. It was not at all clear whether she would prove herself a genius, or merely quite good. Writing to Violet Dickinson, the first real love of her life, she laid out her position at the crossroads: 'I shall be miserable, or happy; a wordy sentimental creature, or a writer of such English as shall one day burn the pages.'[1] Four years later, her dreams had eluded her. She sent her sister Vanessa a simple, desolate summing up: 'to be 29 and unmarried – to be a failure – childless – insane too, no writer'.[2] But she had not given up. In that same letter she saw her pages burning. It was June and there had been a thunderstorm. She was full of fire and eroticism. Even as she announced her failure, she felt her language flaring up: 'every word glows like a horseshoe on the anvil with passion'.[3]

She went on to become one of the greatest writers of all time. Today she is celebrated not only for her novels but for her essays, her social polemics, her memoirs, her experiments in biography, her glittering and moving diaries, and her many, many letters. The story of her life is one of determination, hard work, and untiring interest in the world around her. She took nothing for granted, from her doubts in 1907 about whether she would be a novelist at all to her conviction that *Between the Acts* was a failure. She could never bank on her own success because she never did the same thing twice.

Her imagery of burning and glowing is romantic, and there was much that was romantic about Virginia Woolf.

Sometimes, in a kind of vision, she would suddenly see the whole shape of a novel. But novels are not written in visions. They are written hour after hour, deleted, despaired of, corrected, and typed out all over again. Reading chronologically through Woolf's diaries and letters, it is possible to put hindsight temporarily on hold and appreciate the decisions she made day by day. Should she stay in Richmond or go back to London? Should she let Vita Sackville-West into her life? She buys a house in the south of France and nearly moves there; she revels in her writing of *The Years* before she falters near the end and it becomes a nightmare. We can flick ahead and see that she will recover from a breakdown and finish a masterpiece, but Woolf's remarkable toughness and tenacity become more apparent when we remember that she, of course, could not.

In this short book I have tried to present in a concise form the outline of Woolf's life and some of the most distinctive patterns of her thought. It is meant as a first port of call for those new to Woolf and as an enticement to read more. I hope it will also set off a few fresh ideas (or arguments) in readers long familiar with the material I present. The body of specialist Woolf scholarship grows ever richer. With every passing year there appear more superb soundings of the archives, exegeses of particular themes, and excavations of historical context. But the telescope as well as the microscope has its role. The short survey can allow new things to stand clear. Its demands on the writer and reader are different but no less intense.

Every reading of Woolf will vary in its emphases; in Woolf's phrase 'the accent falls differently from of old'.[4] My own accents here are provisional, and I expect in future I shall want to move them. Last year I would have said more about art and about Roger Fry. This year, rereading *To the Lighthouse*, I could not stop thinking about its religious iconography and atheism. Reading Woolf's novels in quick succession, I saw more clearly than before the spirit of *Orlando* in all of them and watched the fun and fantasy getting into some of the darkest corners. Woolf noted once that she missed 'the glow & the flattery & the festival' of Vita.[5] Through much of the reading for this book, it seemed to me that Woolf was her own festival, and her work an extraordinary celebration of life. There is much that is controversial about Woolf, much that one may want to criticize and debate. But, whatever else she does, she makes one want to live more consciously and fully.

Soon after my first encounter with *To the Lighthouse* as a teenager, I read Hermione Lee's biography of Woolf. It was the book that showed me what literature can do and sent me off to study English. Lee shaped my responses to Woolf very early on and continues to do so, which means that this short study is indebted to her *Virginia Woolf* in too many ways to number. I can only record my deepest thanks and hope that I have not trespassed too far. I would also like to thank the many other writers on Woolf whose work appears in the 'Notes' and 'Suggestions for Further Reading' and from whom I have learned what I know. My warmest thanks to Lara Feigel and Felicity James for their acute comments on my text, and to my agent Caroline Dawnay for her conviction. I am deeply grateful to Jamie Camplin, and to everyone at Thames & Hudson who has worked on this book. Special thanks must go to my editor Amanda Vinnicombe, copy-editor Richard Dawes, picture editor Mary-Jane Gibson, and to Andrew Brown for the index. I very much appreciate the support of those who have allowed me to quote work in copyright, details of which are given at the end of the book. Lastly, thanks to Robert Harris as ever, to Jane Lewis who first took me to Monk's House as a student, and to my own students at the University of Liverpool who got more Woolf than they had bargained for and then chose to read even more.

Virginia Stephen at twenty, photographed by George Beresford in 1902.

Who was I then? Adeline Virginia Stephen, the second daughter of Leslie and Julia Prinsep Stephen, born on 25th January 1882, descended from a great many people, some famous, others obscure; born into a large connection, born not of rich parents but of well-to-do parents, born into a very communicative, literate, letter writing, visiting, articulate, late nineteenth century world [...]

Virginia Woolf, 'Sketch of the Past', 18 April 1939

1   Victorians   1882–1895

There were already a great many people at 22 Hyde Park Gate in Kensington when Virginia Stephen was born in the big marital bedroom on the first floor. Her parents, Julia and Leslie Stephen, each had children from a previous marriage. Gerald and George were Julia's sons from her marriage to Herbert Duckworth, away at school for much of the time, but always welcomed home with tearful ceremony. Julia's daughter Stella, twelve when Virginia was born, was a fixed part of the household and an important figure in the Stephen children's lives. Then there was Leslie's daughter Laura, who was a troubling, unknowable presence in the house, chattering wildly, 'vacant-eyed',[1] a source of painful anxiety to Leslie, who did not know what was wrong with her or how to help. Up in the nursery Virginia was among her siblings: her elder sister Vanessa, born in 1879, her brother Thoby, born in 1880, and Adrian, the youngest of them all, born in 1883. A middle-class family of this size needed servants. There was the family's long-standing cook Sophie Farrell, and seven maids who had their bedrooms in the attic and a sitting room down in the gloom of the basement.

The narrow building strained to accommodate all these lives, each with its demands and complications. And in this house the strain was especially noticeable because alongside the living there were the letters, mementoes, and memories of all the family's dead. Virginia was named after Aunt Adeline who had just died, though the 'Adeline' was quickly dropped because it made Julia so sad. The happiness of Leslie and Julia's marriage was founded on their shared sense of lost first loves. They both believed in the art of remembering, and every corner of their house was full of stories.

Looking back, Hyde Park Gate seemed to Virginia 'so crowded with scenes of family life, grotesque, comic and tragic; with the violent emotions of youth, revolt, despair, intoxicating happiness, immense boredom' that just to sit and recollect it all seemed suffocating. Everything was so 'tangled and matted with emotion'.[2] Julia's taste in furnishing emphasized the darkness and fullness: 'mounds of plush, Watts' portraits, busts shrined in crimson velvet'.[3] The drawing room was sub-divided by black-painted folding doors, which, Virginia remembered, determined the whole rhythm of the house. There might be a crisis on one side of the door and a cheerful Sunday tea on the other. One might be expected to emerge from a painful conversation on the 'secret' side and immediately start entertaining the visitors eating buns on the other.[4] Everything depended on the effort at containment, but inevitably the mood of one room impinged on the next.

This pattern of things contained or spilling over would keep coming back in Woolf's fiction right up to her last novel *Between the Acts*, where a mood is 'brewed up' then interrupted and spilled.[5] When Woolf wrote about early childhood in *The Waves* she recorded the intense private perceptions of different children ('I see a ring'; 'I hear a sound'; 'I see a crimson tassel'), but then she recorded the shock of those moments when the envelope of individual consciousness is punctured by sudden awareness of other people: people with secret feelings of their own.[6] As a child she was struck repeatedly by this realization of separate, unknown lives. There might be the news that someone had proposed in the garden; or just a look in her mother's eye that suggested hidden emotion. She would always remember Julia returning from the bedside of a local man she had been nursing: 'I was playing. I stopped, about to speak to her. But she half turned from us, and lowered her eyes.'[7] Virginia did not need to be told that the man had died.

When Virginia Woolf tried to recover distinct images of her mother, the figure was often looking away. But she was nonetheless the central magnetic force in all the children's lives. Julia Stephen was a gracious, melancholy beauty, the muse of Pre-Raphaelite painters, the white-draped Madonna of Burne-Jones's *The Annunciation* (painted in 1879 when she was pregnant with Vanessa), the haunting face in the photographs taken by her aunt Julia Margaret Cameron, who allowed the ink to blur at the edges so that the hooded eyes and high, hollow cheeks seem those of an apparition.[8] Julia was the mythologized subject of these Victorian dreams, and at the same time she was a practical and extremely hard-working woman with a large family to look after and a commitment to nursing anyone whose need came to her attention, whether rich or poor, relative or stranger. Not without cause had she warned Leslie when they became engaged that she would devote much of her life to her work. But she was good at entertainment too, and though the Victorian painters were not inclined to show their Madonnas having fun, Julia was responsible for much family merriment. The adult Virginia, whose friends often commented on her wild laughter, thought she had inherited her mother's hooting laugh.

Because Julia was always busy, Virginia was aware of her more as a 'general presence' than a 'particular person'.[9] It was a presence Woolf would feel for the rest of her life, and she would keep trying to understand who this powerful, complicated woman was. Mrs Ramsay in *To the Lighthouse* creates an atmosphere and a centre of gravity, but though she is meant to

Julia Stephen with a young Virginia, 1884. One of Virginia's very earliest memories, recorded in 'Sketch of the Past', was of sitting with her mother: 'red and purple flowers on a black ground – my mother's dress; and she was sitting either in a train or in an omnibus, and I was on her lap'.

be sitting for her portrait, she moves her head to tend to her son and her visitors. It is very hard for Lily Briscoe to paint her.

While Julia was supporting the panoply of family life, or out on exhausting rounds of visiting, Leslie Stephen was in his study at the top of the house. Here he wrote the books that made him a major figure of nineteenth-century culture: literary criticism, philosophy, history, biography. In the year of Virginia's birth he exchanged the editorship of the *Cornhill Magazine* for an even larger project, *The Dictionary of National Biography*, a monumental record of the nation's great public figures. He had to organize the work of more than 600 contributors, and he himself researched and wrote 378 of the entries. It was an enormous strain. He was seized with anxiety and couldn't sleep at night; during the day the children would hear loud groans from his study, and when he emerged his mood could be foul. Too often he called in aid a certain nineteenth-century cult of male genius which allowed for fits of rage and inspiration. Nevertheless, when he paused from work he could be delightful and attentive to his children, helping them to catch butterflies in the garden, telling them about his energetic Alpine expeditions, reading aloud to them, or asking after their own reading.

His was 'only a good second class mind', he ruefully told his clever young daughter.[10] But she would go on admiring what he wrote and respecting the free-thinking intellectual integrity that made him speak out as an atheist and a rationalist. Reading his books, as she did at intervals right up to her death, gave her a way of continuing her relationship with him. Julia, by contrast, had left nothing so solid and reliable behind. Who was she then? Did it matter that she left so little physical trace? This is one of the questions that keeps being asked in *To the Lighthouse*. What will last? For Virginia Woolf, writing was a counter to transience. If you wrote something down, you could make it stay put.

Sir Leslie Stephen by G. F. Watts, 1878. This melancholy and distinguished
portrait, commissioned by Leslie as an engagement present for Julia, was
part of the atmosphere of Hyde Park Gate.

She felt this from very early on, and there was certainly a good deal of writing being done up in the nursery. Every Monday without fail from 1892, when Virginia was ten, she and Vanessa, sometimes Thoby too, delivered to their parents the *Hyde Park Gate News*. This illustrated newspaper (now collected and published) records the competitive, industrious life of the Stephen children.[11] Everyone had a gamut of nicknames and roles to play. There were fierce debates over domestic occurrences, and no visitor to the house escaped without having been privately assessed and caricatured.

Twice a day the children were taken for an airing in Kensington Gardens. This grew understandably tedious, though Virginia was wide awake and noticed everything: the old woman at the Queen's Gate who sold nuts and boot laces, the little ribbed shells along the Flower Walk. There was usually something newsworthy to report, and when there wasn't Virginia would write a story. Because she had a lot to say, it would often be a very long story, issued in weekly instalments.

What were these ambitious editors of the *Hyde Park Gate News* going to do with their lives? The future that Julia Stephen envisaged for her daughters was one of distinguished domestic activity. They would be wives, mothers, supports, carers. Traditional in her thinking about women's roles and firmly opposed to women's suffrage, Julia saw no need for her daughters to have a formal education. In this she was not especially conservative: with a few rare exceptions, girls in the 1890s simply did not go out to school. Leslie might have allowed his children to be the rare exceptions, but instead he accepted his wife's judgment on the matter. So Thoby and Adrian went off to school and later to Cambridge. Vanessa and Virginia remained at home.

Their parents made a huge and sustained effort to provide the tuition and encouragement the children needed. Julia sat them down for lessons when she could, but she had other demands on her time. Leslie taught them maths, introduced them to the classics, and supplied books from his library. Both were principled and capable educators, but they could not give the structure and consistency available at school. Nor could they provide the sociable company of peers. The sisters kept company with each other.

Virginia seems always to have known that she was going to be a writer. And Vanessa knew she was going to be a painter.[12] This was sorted out very early on, and they proceeded to train themselves competitively in their chosen arts. For years Virginia persisted in using a writing table so high that she had to stand up. This gave a formality and seriousness to what she was doing, and it put her on an equal footing with Vanessa, who would be standing at her easel. So the two girls stood, hour after hour, in their room on the third floor of the house. They were absolutely determined: they were going to make their way.

For nine months of the year London was the backdrop to Virginia's life. But when the adult Virginia Woolf thought about her childhood, what she often thought of before anything else was a garden by the sea. It was a garden of intense sensory experience, of voices in the dusk and hedges you could peer through to the world beyond: 'through the pear-shaped leaves of the escallonia, fishing boats seemed caught and suspended'.[13]

This is the garden of Talland House in St Ives, where Virginia Stephen spent her first thirteen summers. Leslie had found the house, with its pretty trelliswork, tall windows, and views to the sea, while on a walking trip in Cornwall. He immediately rented it for family holidays, despite the difficulties of getting three babies and a whole household down there each year. Still, in a letter of 1884 we hear the voice of a proud, excited father. He was enchanted by the garden with its flowering hedges and 'remote nooks' and 'high banks, down which you can slide in a sitting posture'. It was, he thought, 'altogether a pocket-paradise with a sheltered cove of sand in easy reach (for 'Ginia even) just below'.[14] And he was right. His daughter would remember and write about it as a kind of paradise for the rest of her life.

Talland House was the scene of what Virginia Woolf described in 1939 as her 'most important memory'. It was the memory, she felt, on which all her others were built:

> It is of lying half asleep, half awake, in bed in the nursery at St Ives. It is of hearing the waves breaking, one, two, one, two, and sending a splash of water over the beach; and then breaking, one, two, one, two, behind a yellow blind. It is of hearing the blind draw its little acorn across the floor as the wind blew the blind out. It is of lying and hearing this splash and seeing this light, and feeling, it is almost impossible that I should be here; of feeling the purest ecstasy I can conceive.[15]

This is a memory of being safe and still, while acutely aware of the great world beyond. Familiar surroundings seem for a moment to be almost miraculous. The rhythm here is the rhythm that sounds through *The Waves* and through Woolf's greatest writing. Nothing outward happens: no one standing at the nursery door and observing the scene would have known its importance. It is one of those hidden revelations that Woolf's fiction would propose as the structuring principles of our lives.

The long summers at St Ives, which lasted from August to October, yielded many of these intense moments of private sensation and lone adventure. There was a circle of safety, and there were exciting, frightening explorations beyond it. Little Jacob in *Jacob's Room* finds himself lost on the beach all alone, and everything looks enormous. He sees two large red faces staring up at him from the sand. 'Jacob stared down at them. Holding his bucket very carefully, Jacob then jumped deliberately and trotted away very nonchalantly at first', but then 'faster and faster', towards safety.[16] Bernard and Susan in *The Waves* are 'discoverers of an unknown land' as they peer over a wall to see the white house between the trees.[17] They look in awe, stowing away an image they will keep, before scrambling in terror back within bounds.

At Talland House, the garden itself was a busy place, and mapped out accordingly. By common consent there were social areas and romantic corners. A game of cricket was usually underway on the lawn, continuing late into the dusk with a fluorescent ball that could just about be seen against the dark hedge. (Virginia's childhood passion for cricket anticipated her adult addiction to bowls.) There was a special system for meeting visitors:

> The Lookout place was a grassy mound, that jutted out
> over the high garden wall. There we were often sent
> to stand to look out for the fall of the signal. When the
> signal fell it was time to start for the station to meet
> the train. It was the train that brought Mr Lowell, Mr
> Gibbs, the Stillmans, the Lushingtons, the Symondses.[18]

In 1894 a hotel was built in front of Talland House, blocking the view to the sea. In September the Stephens packed up their holiday home for the last time, though they didn't know it. That autumn Julia became ill with rheumatic fever. She was only forty-eight, but in photographs from that last year she

Virginia and Vanessa Stephen at St Ives, 1894. A great deal of cricket was
played in the garden at Talland House, and Virginia was notorious as a bowler.
Later, she and Leonard would regularly play highly competitive bowls.

looks drawn and exhausted. The expert on sickbeds was herself now in need of nursing. In *To the Lighthouse* the narrative lingers over the empty holiday house where draughts creep in and lift the edges of possessions left behind: a cloak, a child's bucket. And then two sentences in brackets report what has happened far away:

> [Mr Ramsay stumbling along a passage stretched his arms out one dark morning, but Mrs Ramsay having died rather suddenly the night before, he stretched his arms out. They remained empty.][19]

There is no report of what the children felt.

Julia Stephen died in London on 5 May 1895. The elaborate routines of Victorian mourning began. 'Rooms were shut', Virginia remembered. 'People were creeping in and out.'[20] Flowers piled up 'reeking' in the hall. Stella, at twenty-six, began stoically to take control. Letters were written on black-edged paper. Leslie sat distraught and groaning in the dark sitting room where thick creeper grew over the windows and kept out the light.

All her life Virginia would try to find ways to express what she felt through all this. In her 1937 novel *The Years*, she took the perspective of the bereaved daughter Delia, who sees that people have started to kneel reverentially at the bedside and that even the nurses are crying.

> Ought I to kneel too? she wondered. Not in the passage, she decided. She looked away; she saw the little window at the end of the passage. Rain was falling; there was a light somewhere that made the raindrops shine. One drop after another slid down the pane; they slid and they paused; one drop joined another drop and then they slid again.[21]

In this series of detached, mechanically registered impressions, the raindrops are suggestive of tears. But importantly they are not tears. The most distressing thing about this time was that Virginia Stephen could not feel what she thought she was meant to be feeling. Though she whispered like the others, on the inside of all this conventionalized public mourning was a numbness potentially more troubling than expressible grief. 'I said to myself as I have done at moments of crisis since, "I feel nothing whatever." '[22] She was indistinctly aware of a mismatch between outer expectation and inner experience. Not until much later could she articulate it. 'It made one hypocritical and enmeshed in the conventions of sorrow', she wrote in her memoir 'Sketch of the Past'. 'We were made to act parts that we did not feel; to fumble for words that we did not know.'[23]

In her fiction she would find ways to break open those conventions. She would insist that the moment of importance comes not 'here' where society demands it, but 'there' when we least expect it. We do not feel things on time, to order. Woolf would license numbness, and she would acknowledge the strange, indirect ways in which people respond to events; she would give credence to the individuality of experience. But at thirteen she found herself hemmed in and overwhelmed.

2   Getting Through   1896–1904

In the months after her mother's death Virginia Stephen was extremely nervous and agitated. Her pulse raced; Leslie and Stella worried about her and consulted doctors. She was told to stop her lessons and rest, but the resting was restless and the tension went on and on. Writing much later, near the end of a life punctuated by intervals of illness, Virginia Woolf identified this episode of 1895–6 as the first of her 'breakdowns'.[1] Her work would help to redefine what that word meant.

What struck her most forcefully, looking back, was that for those two years after Julia's death she read and read but did not write. 'The desire left me; which I have had all my life, with that two years break.'[2] There would be other periods when she could not write. When her voluble and amazingly energetic diary goes silent, as it does for months at a time, it is because she was unable – or was not allowed by her doctors – to record her usual flights of imaginative response to the world. Since she wrote very little during her breakdowns, our sense of what she experienced comes mostly from the reports of others and from the way she wrote about mental illness in her fiction.

Most, though not all, of her symptoms were those of manic depression, now also known as bipolar disorder.[3] There were moments of vivid, ecstatic perception, overwhelming emotions that could change very quickly, a great fear of public exposure, and the exhaustion of overspent nervous energy. This was the illness which would become part of her life: watched for, scrutinized, darkly fascinating to her, hated, and battled through. Today millions of people are taking mood-stabilizing drugs to help limit the extremes of mania and depression. In 1896 all that could be prescribed was rest and sedatives (which may well have made things worse). There were frightening things in store if she did not improve; her half-sister Laura would spend most of her life undiagnosed in a series of asylums. Madness was close to home and absolutely terrifying. Virginia Stephen did not want it, and she felt for her own ways of surviving.

One of the signs of her recovery was that in the New Year of 1897, just before her fifteenth birthday, she started to keep a journal. It is the most fully recorded year of her childhood, a day-by-day account of the routine pleasures and trials of Hyde Park Gate. The most frequently repeated words in the diary are 'Nessa went to drawing.' This is how she starts her entry for each of the days on which Vanessa went off to her morning classes at art school. Virginia chronicled her own life at this lonely time in relation to her sister's absence. Her brothers were away at school and she was the one left behind. But she had her own work to do.

Virginia was allowed to take lessons again and now had private tuition in Greek. In the mornings, between ten and one, she sat up in her room reading books lent to her by her father from his library. Leslie was consciously guiding her towards his own profession as a historian and biographer, so the reading list was full of Froude and Macaulay and Carlyle. She went through all these at rapacious speed, daily returning to her father for another volume, sometimes being sent back upstairs to slow down and read yesterday's book again.

In the afternoons there would be errands and excursions in London with Stella or Vanessa, and often a stop for buns at an ABC teashop. It was an 1890s upper-middle-class childhood

Adrian and Virginia Stephen on holiday at Fritham in 1900. Their relationship would always be an uneasy one, and it is difficult to interpret because their letters have not survived. When they shared houses in their twenties, they irritated and disappointed each other. Woolf pitied his seeming vulnerability; it was not until Adrian was in his forties and established as a psychoanalyst that she thought he looked settled and ready to begin.

of visits and chores and small entertainments. But in every spare moment Virginia Stephen read. As well as the ten-to-one morning books, there were 'supper and odd moment books', even designated hair-brushing books.[4] Last thing at night she would take a book to bed with her, though this was not strictly allowed. Her 'nightly forbidden reading' had to be furtive; she squirrelled the volume away when she heard anyone approaching.[5] This secrecy was all part of the literary seduction.

And seduction it was. She loved the feel of books – their bindings and typefaces. Once one got between the covers, whole new adventures in feeling were begun. She read on her own, but her passion for reading was part of her passion for other people. So when Leslie gave her for her birthday a ten-volume *Life of Walter Scott*, she was in thrall to its beauty and all it signified about her father's respect for her. Reading was also, quite practically and literally, a means of survival. Virginia learned how to use it to stabilize herself when she felt the 'agitation', the 'fidgets', and mood swings that were a part of her illness.[6] She learned this out of necessity during these difficult years.

In April 1897 Stella married her long-time admirer Jack Hills. Leslie was aghast at the idea that she might leave home, seeing quite rightly that the house would fall apart without her. In the end, she moved a few doors down the street so that she could continue as the central support for the Stephen children. But even this carefully negotiated arrangement, which was very trying for Stella, could not protect the Stephen family from disaster. Stella returned seriously ill from her honeymoon and within three months she was dead. The children were again left without a maternal figure. Leslie was again left without the female help and sympathy that he seemed uncontrollably to need.

Assiduously writing her diary as all this went on, Virginia chose not to pour out her unhappiness. Instead she wrote sharp-witted, opinionated descriptions of her world. It was a way of keeping herself up on the surface of life. The daily round of walks, visits, tea and buns might have been monotonous, but writing it out helped her to 'plod on'.[7] 'Life is a hard business –' she reflected in October, 'one needs a rhinirocerous [sic] skin – & that one has not got.'[8] To the end of her life she would be wishing for that tough skin, observing for a pleasing moment in 1937, for example, that reviewers' comments on *The Years* affected her no more than 'tickling a rhinoceros with a feather'.[9] Most of the time she felt herself to be porous, tickled by the lightest feather, constantly receiving and responding to jolts.

One of the worst consequences of Stella's death was the change it brought in the behaviour of her brother George Duckworth, who now, in his early thirties, tried to establish himself as head of the household. He did for the Stephen sisters what he probably thought were the right things: he took them out and showed them off, bought them presents, and made histrionic displays of his affection for them. The affection was not returned in equal measure. Though Virginia felt some fondness for her half-brother (she had grown up with 'dearest Georgie' and when he died in 1934 she would feel the 'glow' of childhood go with him), she also felt contempt.[10] She and Vanessa loathed his stupidity and felt acutely the injustice of being lorded over by a dim-witted social climber who had no understanding of what mattered to them. George tried to make Virginia love him, and then his version of 'love' got out of control.

Earlier, when she was six or seven, her other half-brother Gerald had intrusively explored her body. She remembered 'resenting, disliking it – what is the word for so dumb and mixed a feeling?'[11] She associated this with the lifelong shame she felt about her body, and which persisted despite her beauty. She would always feel anxious about mirrors and awkward about clothes. What George did between about 1897 and 1904 was much more sustained than Gerald's touching. But we do not know what form it took or how often it happened. Least of all do we know how far these violations shaped Virginia's life and work, though a great deal has been written on the subject.[12] We are reliant on accounts she gave at various later stages: in autobiographical sketches from 1908 and 1939, in a few letters, and in two papers read to the Bloomsbury Group's Memoir Club in the 1920s which were designed to intrigue and entertain. Though 'Bloomsbury' came to pride itself on sexual candour, none of these accounts is explicit about what George did when he crept into Virginia's bedroom and told her not to turn on the light.

She says much more about his stupidity than about his sexuality. The physical intrusion was linked up with a threatened dimming and blunting of her mind. Virginia tried to reduce her horror of George by turning him into a joke with Vanessa, and between them they made him a figure of pitiful fun. He had 'animal vigour', Virginia wrote in 1908, but not enough brain to control it: 'he allowed himself to commit acts which a cleverer man would have called tyrannical; and, profoundly believing in the purity of his love, he behaved little better than a brute.'[13] By 1921 she was ending her Memoir Club talk with a provocative flourish: 'the old ladies of Kensington and Belgravia never knew that George Duckworth was not only father and mother, brother and sister to those poor Stephen girls; he was their lover also'.[14] What is the tone here? Was the audience meant to laugh at this dramatic ending to a comic paper about George's snobbery and ridiculousness? Woolf was testing her own reactions too, mastering the different tones in which she could present to others – and to herself – what had happened.

The humiliations in the dark would always be connected for her with the public humiliation she felt when George took her out into the high society he revered. Vanessa had suffered enough evenings on George's arm and put her foot down. George turned to Virginia, who gave the social round a try. There were balls and dinners, tiaras, titles, all the huge wealth of late-Victorian aristocracy. Her face fitted, but her conversation did not. She was meant to give short, pretty responses to the questions she was asked, but instead she talked about Plato, realized she had broken the code, blushed, shut up, and despaired. Though in her accounts of these parties she says she was hopeless at small talk, it is hard to believe that she could not have pulled it off with cunning aplomb.[15] Had she played the prescribed part, this could have been her world. But she was not going to do it.

Thirty years later, when society hostesses like Lady Sibyl Colefax chased the celebrity author for her guest lists, Woolf would play hard to get. It was a pleasing sequel to her embarrassments with George that she was eventually invited, in her own right and on her own terms, to shine centre stage. She would protest about having to waste time at these parties, but there was always, too, something in them that she found alluring. She recorded their rituals with fascination and she grasped the point of the superficiality. Parties made people behave in a way that matched their thin silk dresses, she observed when she was twenty-one: 'for two or three hours a number of people have resolved to show only their silken side to one another'.[16] She could see that beneath this willed coherence parties had their own reality and depth. 'It was possible to say things you couldn't say anyhow else, things that needed an effort; possible to go much deeper', Clarissa thinks in *Mrs Dalloway*, the novel in which Virginia Woolf paid tribute to the society woman she did not become.[17] She saw the composed party as a kind of art.

It was not her art, but she would give it its due, while returning at the same time, through the character of Septimus Warren-Smith, to the dreadful feelings of exposure and powerlessness that originated at those parties with George.

It was not that everything before Julia's death was happy and everything after it was not, although this was the broad pattern things took in Virginia Woolf's memory. She came to regard the period from 1897 to 1904, her whole adolescence from the age of fifteen to twenty-two, as 'the seven unhappy years', but there were still some pleasures to be found.[18] It was a time of intimacy and shared understanding with Vanessa, which made home life tolerable. It was also a time of making friends. Generous, varied, and passionate friendship is one of the great stories of her life and she began it now by forging intense relationships with women. From her cousins Emma and Madge Vaughan, and from her tutor Janet Case, she won the affection she badly needed. And she gave in return the overwhelming affection she needed to give.

There were still family holidays. Leslie could not bear to see St Ives again after Julia's death (he could not bring himself to return as Mr Ramsay does, to make the postponed journey to the lighthouse; Virginia Woolf would have to imagine that act of reparation). But each year a house in the country was rented for the summer. Though they never possessed Virginia's imagination as Talland House did, they would be sensuously remembered. The family Entomological Society (President: Leslie Stephen; Secretary: Virginia Stephen) was still devoted to its twilight work of moth catching. Virginia still felt the magic of torchlit gardens, the rituals of sugaring the branches in expectation, the beauty of the creatures caught momentarily in the light. At Warboys in Cambridgeshire one night in the summer of 1899, the lantern illuminated a Red Underwing and

Virginia caught it in her notebook as well as in the sugar:

> By the faint glow we could see the huge moth – his
> wings open, as though in ecstasy, so that the splendid
> crimson of the underwing could be seen – his eyes
> burning red, his proboscis plunged into a flowing stream
> of treacle. We gazed one moment on his splendour,
> & then uncorked the bottle.[19]

Alone or with others, there were long cycle rides and
skating in winter, and a lot of vigorous walking by which
Virginia proved herself the daughter of Leslie Stephen the
famously robust Alpine mountaineer. Even during these tense
'unhappy years' she was often to be found striding through
Kensington Square to her Greek class or writing a wicked
mock-eighteenth-century sketch of some visiting dignitary.
She was undertaking, day by day and of her own accord, a pro-
gramme of education that meant she could hold her own with
any learned don or literary light who came her way. When
Thoby was at home, they talked literature together and she
loved it, but then he went away again. She wanted his opinions
about Shakespeare, Marlowe, Sophocles, and she wanted to
get the better of him. But: 'Oh dear oh dear – just as I feel in
the mood to talk about these things, you go and plant your-
self in Cambridge.'[20] She carried on without him. At twenty
she was absorbed by Greek drama, Renaissance travel writing,
and eighteenth-century prose; and she was attending at King's
College Women's Department as many lectures as she could.

Almost everything she wrote as an adult is shaped in some
way by the fundamental fact of her not having been to school
or university. She would come to fashion herself defiantly as an
'outsider', exploiting the unorthodox vantage points it gave her.
She would take the side of the 'common reader' while attacking

Thoby Stephen, Virginia's elder brother, ally, and confidant. His friends at Cambridge would become her friends, and his image would later haunt her novels. He was photographed by George Beresford in 1906 just before leaving for Italy and Greece.

the pomp and exclusivity of academia. In her essays she would develop a style based on informal conversation rather than systematic analysis; she preferred to wander or 'ramble' round her subject rather than attack it head-on, and as a literary critic she would more often write about the impressions, tastes, and textures of a book than about its hard facts.[21]

This liberated and original voice took time and confidence to develop. Virginia Stephen had first to train herself in literary styles. She set herself exercises, filling notebooks 'as an artist fills his pages with scraps & fragments'.[22] There were cloud studies and portraits of people, views of buildings, scenes at parties. She was desperate for someone to read all this and to love her for it. The person she found was Violet Dickinson, a kind, intelligent, well-connected, extremely tall (six foot two), widely loved, and contentedly unmarried woman seventeen years her senior. Visiting Hyde Park Gate, Violet saw that the Stephen girls needed an older woman to turn to, but it was with Virginia particularly that she made a connection. They were conscious of making up the relationship as they went along, pushing it beyond the close companionship that was very common among women towards something that more resembled a love affair. 'I cant think how one writes to an intimate friend,' Virginia protested, but she was not held up for long.[23] Through 1902–3 her letters to Violet were alive with sensuality. Often a tranche of her latest writing was enclosed which became part of the love letter. As in all the intimate relationships of her life, she invented animal characters that allowed her an erotic language of nuzzling and cuddling. She took the temperature of Violet's letters in return and demanded that they get hotter.

Virginia Stephen's other critical relationship at this time was with her father. Her feelings towards him were extremely strong and conflicted. It was he who understood her intellect and believed seriously in her future as a writer. But since Julia's death he had been mired in his own grief and prone to self-indulgent outbursts that made Hyde Park Gate feel as claustrophobic as a cage. His deafness exacerbated his sense of isolation and injustice. Something of his mood can be gleaned from the memoir he wrote during these years.[24] It was a complex mix of self-reproach, self-justification, and mythologizing of two lost wives. This was all intended for his children as part of their inheritance, though few would have seen this weight of grief and guilt as an heirloom they would want to pass on. The children jokingly christened it the *Mausoleum Book*. Leslie was diagnosed with cancer in 1902 and spent a long time dying. It seemed to be going on for ever.

And then it all ended in a night when Leslie Stephen died in February 1904. Vanessa was full of relief. Virginia, years later, said it was a mercy he had not lived into old age. 'His life would have entirely ended mine. What would have happened? No writing, no books; –inconceivable.'[25] This was the great release that allowed her a life of her own, but first she nearly died of it. She was dangerously ill from April to September that year. Advised to leave London, she went to live with Violet at Welwyn in Hertfordshire, where she made at least one attempt to kill herself. She raged against Vanessa, whose zest for life seemed callous in the face of Leslie's death.

Virginia's way of regaining some stability was not to forget but to think very intently about her father. She was asked to help the historian Frederic Maitland with the research for his biography of Leslie, so she went to Cambridge for the autumn to read and transcribe hundreds of family letters. She also contributed a 'Note' to the biography, which absorbed her for weeks as she agonized about getting it right.[26] This was an early exploration of the possibility that writing about the past might be a powerful and positive way of setting it to rest.

Virginia and Leslie Stephen, photographed by George Beresford in
December 1902. Virginia loved, admired, and battled with her father
until the end of his life. She kept rereading and rewriting him until the
end of hers.

Meanwhile in London, what had once seemed impossible now happened. Vanessa cleared out thirty years of accumulated family belongings at Hyde Park Gate, the whole archaeology of relics (Herbert Duckworth's old barrister's wig; tin boxes of letters; hoards of china), and set up a home for the Stephen siblings at a house she had chosen in Bloomsbury. For an awful moment George decided that he was coming too, but they were saved: George got married and went his way. Virginia came back to London briefly in November, sat at her desk with a big new inkpot, and secured her first commission (through Violet) to write an essay and book reviews for a clerical newspaper called the *Guardian*. She arranged her new study as she wanted it: 'all my beloved leather backed books standing up so handsome in their shelves, and a nice fire, and the electric light burning, and a huge mass of manuscripts and letters'.[27] This was going to be a writer's room.

The Stephens went in high spirits to Hampshire for a Christmas break. Virginia wrote long, energetic letters, full of the old addiction to language: 'when I see a pen and ink, I cant help taking to it, as some people do to gin'.[28] Then on New Year's Day 1905 she looked up hopefully at the sky. It was bright and clear, 'as though we had turned over a new leaf & swept the sky clean of clouds'.[29] She could feel herself beginning again; she even persuaded herself she could smell spring in the air. 'I want to work like a steam engine', she wrote to Violet.[30] She kept using images her father might have used (Leslie likened Carlyle to a steam engine and liked to 'get drunk intellectually'), and she was going to prove that she too could be a great essayist and thinker.[31] A few days later she went back to London to make a start. And on 10 January something satisfying arrived in the post as payment for her first published work: 'Found this morning on my plate my first instalment of wages – £2.7.6.'[32]

3   Setting Up   1905–1915

The house in Gordon Square was large and bright. With no figure of authority to set out the rules, it seemed that new patterns of life could be invented here. Thoby and his friends from Cambridge sat up late in the drawing room; Vanessa was revelling in the sense of liberation. The scene was set for the sexual, social, and artistic freedoms that would become associated with 'Bloomsbury'. Virginia would later enjoy talking about this great moment of release. Gordon Square was 'the most beautiful, the most exciting, the most romantic place in the world', she told the Memoir Club in the 1920s, doing her bit to establish the cultural legend: 'everything was going to be new; everything was going to be different. Everything was on trial.'[1]

At the time, however, she was not so sure about it. She walked sadly around Regent's Park, comparing it with Kensington Gardens. She was not convinced about the new friends either. They seemed rather silent, and when they talked it was all very abstract. They were easy to satirize: Virginia noted that 'occasionally they escape to a corner and chuckle over a Latin joke'.[2] She felt herself to be different from them, but she caricatured herself as well. 'I went to a dance last night,' she told Violet in January 1906, 'and found a dim corner where I sat and read In Memoriam.'[3] It was her wry shorthand for her sense of being at odds with a world she was

Vanessa Bell, *The Bedroom, Gordon Square*, 1912. When the Stephens
moved to Bloomsbury they felt that 'everything was going to be different'.
New ways of living developed in tandem with new forms of art.

meant to be enjoying, a comically morose figure still mired in Victorian mourning and very much aware of the ironies.

She tested her responses to other people, working out how far she wanted company and how often she wanted to be alone. Going back to St Ives with her siblings in the summer of 1905, she was reclaiming, with them, the emotions of a family childhood. But her strongest feelings on that trip came from being alone on solitary tramps of the kind her father always loved. She was taking possession, by herself, of a place she needed. 'The beautiful sights are often melancholy & very lonely', she wrote.[4] She wondered why the group excursions she planned with her siblings to famous beauty spots did not move her so much; she realized that, for her, the really 'special sights' were 'sudden, unexpected, secret'.[5]

For Virginia the first years in Bloomsbury were characterized by plain hard work. She was lecturing at Morley College (then housed at the Old Vic near Waterloo), where she taught history and composition to adults. Nervous about teaching subjects she knew back to front, and never complacent about anything, she expended great effort on preparing her lectures. She didn't much enjoy it though, and it was her journalism that really took off. Word got around that she was a skilled reviewer, and by mid-1905 she was totting up in her journal the large number of articles she had written: pieces on Gissing, James, Thackeray, Dickens, women, 'street music', the art of the essay.[6]

Her longer-term ambition was still to write history, like her father, and her encouraging aunt Caroline suggested a life of Henry VIII. Virginia would look back on the idea with laughter but it wasn't so very far off the mark. What would that unwritten book have been like? Perhaps *Orlando* gives us a clue. In the end she would choose fiction, but all her books explore different ways of writing the past.

Her feeling for history was at its most intense on some of the ambitious journeys abroad that she undertook with friends and family. At Mycenae with her siblings and Violet, her imagination worked archaeologically, digging through strata. In flashes, the ancient world opened up to her. 'I did see, for a second, as through a chink, down, down, for miles beneath my feet.'[7] This trip would become a sad marker in her personal history too. When the party of five arrived back in England, three of them were already seriously ill. Violet went home with typhoid. The Gordon Square house became a domestic hospital, with Thoby and Vanessa upstairs in bed under constant supervision. As the nurses came in and out, Virginia talked anxiously with them in a language of enemas and bedpans. Thoby, it finally emerged, had typhoid too.

Virginia had been here before, except that now she was in charge and on her own. She wanted to talk to Violet, still her 'Mother Wallaby', but when she wrote to Violet, as she did almost daily, she was writing to a sick woman who needed *her* to be the strong one. So she sent long, cheerful, practical reports on her patients' ups and downs, encouraging and nursing Violet too, by post. The fates of the three people closest to Virginia seemed horribly entwined. If one got through, perhaps they all would. If not... But she did not allow herself that possibility.

Thoby died on 20 November 1906, aged twenty-nine. Virginia had to write letters and arrange his affairs; but over the next month she also wrote one of her most extraordinary fictions. In her letters to Violet, Thoby remained alive, eating whey and chicken broth, reading reviews, being visited by friends. She thought the truth would be too much of a blow for the already vulnerable Violet. To save her, and perhaps also to save herself, she kept Thoby alive. There was something else she kept from Violet because she could not let it happen just yet. Two days after Thoby's death, Vanessa accepted Clive Bell's proposal of marriage and it was agreed that they would live alone together at Gordon Square. Virginia would need to make another life for herself. All of this was held at bay in the intensely imagined world of the letters. Violet found out eventually and forgave Virginia for the lies. Perhaps the ghostly fiction had got them through. 'The earth seems swept very bare', Virginia wrote, with a hint in her image of the Greek tragedies with which she would always associate her lost brother.[8]

While Vanessa and Clive flourished in their married life, Virginia tried to set up a way of living contentedly on her own. She moved with Adrian to Fitzroy Square, but they had never been close and chose to live as independently as possible. Virginia worked hard at her reviewing and took off regularly on trips to the country, roaming as the fancy took her, writing sensuously about it in journals and letters. Out on the Cornish moors and the Sussex Downs, as much as in the 'dim corner' of the party, she was trying out her identity as an eccentric lone thinker. Was that what she wanted to be? She saw a long unmarried future spread before her, the validity of which seemed to depend entirely on her success as a writer. 'I see how I shall spend my days a virgin, an Aunt, an authoress.'[9]

With the arrival of Vanessa's first child, Julian, in February 1908, Virginia felt more than ever an intruder in her sister's maternal 'circle of bliss'.[10] But as Vanessa devoted herself to her baby, Clive too was feeling left out. A dangerous flirtation developed which might have been disastrous for them all. Though she would look back in horror on this episode, Virginia found it difficult at the time to resist the new power it gave her. She let the flattery go too far, but she did not let it become an affair.

As she drew back she needed to prove her independence a virtue. She spent the summer of 1908 at Manorbier in Wales, alone but not lonely. 'I end upon the beach generally, – find a corner where I can sit and invent images from the shapes of the waves.'[11] She was preparing and focusing herself for an intensive period of work on the novel she was writing, which would eventually become *The Voyage Out*. 'I mean to stand at my desk this autumn', she told Clive, 'and work doggedly, in the dark.'[12]

She stylishly played up her role as the mad aunt. At 12.30 on Christmas Eve 1909 she decided to go to Cornwall and made a dash for the one o'clock train. The next day – the day of the year most associated with family – she walked over the hills in the mist and then posted back to London vivid portraits of her triumphantly spontaneous excursion. She wrote to her sister with relish to say that she had run off with 'no pocket handkerchief, watch key, notepaper, spectacles, cheque book, looking glass, or coat' and was now sitting happily over the fire in an empty hotel.[13] As ever, her reading provided the models against which she measured her own behaviour. That Christmas she was zooming 'like an express train' through the multi-volume memoirs of the eccentric Lady Hester Stanhope, who kept forty-eight cats, rode through Syria in trousers, and 'took herself for the Messiah'.[14] Virginia couldn't help imagining herself for a moment as a modern Lady Stanhope. She fired off to Clive a quick fantasy: 'Suppose I stayed here, and thought myself an early virgin, and danced on May nights, [...] a scandalous Aunt for Julian.'[15] So she jokingly, brilliantly weighed future versions of herself.

What she wanted most of all was to finish her novel, but for much of 1910 she was kept away from it. By the end of February, her tension and restlessness was at the dangerous point of tipping over into illness. Dr George Savage advised her to be away from London, and there began a series of trips designed to help her rest. In June, Vanessa rented a house outside Canterbury where she thought she might be able to help her sister recover. But by the end of the month there was no recovery, Virginia felt herself a burden, and Savage prescribed a 'rest cure' at Burley Park hospital in Twickenham. Virginia submitted because it would relieve her heavily pregnant sister, and because – just perhaps – it might work. In her letters at least, she was stoically accepting: '[Savage] says he wont insist on complete isolation, so I suppose I shant be as badly off as I was before.'[16] It was bad nonetheless: she was force-fed, deprived of literature and company, and had no idea of when it might end. She kept testing her brain to see if it was 'ripe' like the harvest, and eventually in the late summer she was able to leave.[17] There was a careful autumn of convalescence in Cornwall and Dorset before she returned tentatively to London.

She was back in time for the opening of 'Manet and the Post-Impressionists', the exhibition that was absorbing all her friends' attention. Its organizer was Roger Fry, an ebullient critic with a passion for modern French painting, who had arrived like a whirlwind in Bloomsbury and made painting the central subject of discussion. The exhibition caused a national sensation; Clive and Vanessa were caught up in a 'sizzle of excitement'.[18]

Virginia was pleased and interested, and her fiction would in time respond with dazzling originality to these debates about art. But she couldn't feel the sizzle the painters felt, and for the moment it seemed that the pictures did not have very much to do with her. 'I dont think them so good as books', she wrote to Violet.[19] And it was an 'awful bore' to dress herself up as a Gauguin muse for the benefit of delighted photographers after the Post-Impressionist Ball.[20] She was not quite sure how she and her writing fitted in. She enlisted Clive as a critic, while sending kisses via him to Vanessa. Really she wanted the praise of her father. She was making something, she was brimming over with it, but she did not know to whom she could give it. 'O to whom?' Rhoda keeps asking in *The Waves*, walking through the world with flowers she has gathered, which she wants to give away.[21]

There was huge pressure to marry. Virginia received no fewer than four proposals, but she couldn't give her life to any of the men who asked. She said 'yes' to her friend Lytton Strachey for a rash moment in February 1909, but by the next day both were thinking better of it. She knew people were discussing her sexuality, and she was made to feel self-conscious as the virgin of her milieu. It felt as if everyone was thinking and talking about bodies: sex, secret affairs, babies, homosexuality, more sex. Her difference from the others showed itself in small ways: when she sat to the painter Francis Dodd for a portrait she knew that she could not pose nude, whereas her sister and her artist friends thought nothing of taking off their clothes.

The small things added up. Madge Vaughan suggested that her writing was too dreamy and lacked 'heart', which sounded to Virginia like a comment on her virginity. She half made a joke of it: 'If marriage is necessary to one's style, I shall have to think about it.'[22] She thought very hard. Watching her sister intently, she played out marriage and motherhood in her mind. ('By the way,' she wrote fiercely to Vanessa, 'I have imagined precisely what it is like to have a child.'[23]) She needed to show she was capable of both, but she wasn't certain she wanted either. For a long time, all through her mid- to late twenties, everything seemed to be at stake.

She was still inventing new domestic arrangements. Wanting more and more to get into the country to read and write in peace, Virginia rented very cheaply a small house under the Sussex Downs, in a landscape she would love for the rest of her life. It would become the Cornwall of her adulthood, and in tribute she called the first of her Sussex homes Little Talland House. Then in the autumn of 1911, after long conversations about 'how to live', she and Adrian exchanged Fitzroy Square for Brunswick Square and set up a kind of lodging house for friends.[24] It was all very carefully and democratically organized, with regular meal times ('trays will be placed in the hall punctually') and rent payments just sufficient to cover expenses.[25] It was also, for these respectable middle-class people, a deeply unconventional way of doing things. Miss Stephen was now the only woman in a house she shared with four men: John Maynard Keynes and Duncan Grant living as a homosexual couple on the ground floor, her brother (who had been Grant's lover) on the first floor, and, in the cheapest rooms at the top of the house, 'a penniless Jew'.[26] Violet, dismayed, found excuses not to visit. Venerable Stephen relatives were alarmed and looked the other way.

There was one other complication: the top-floor lodger was in love with the landlady. Leonard Woolf had been Lytton Strachey's best friend at Cambridge, and part of Thoby Stephen's circle. After university he followed a different course from the others, setting off miserably to Ceylon for a life in the Colonial Service. He disliked the whole system, but he did his work effectively and held on to his imaginative life by writing a novel called *The Village in the Jungle*. He was well launched on a successful career when he returned to London for a year's leave in 1911. Leonard had always found Virginia alluring. Now she trusted him enough to read him her novel, and they talked together about what they wanted for their lives. It was clear that Leonard could not take Virginia to Ceylon, but increasingly he realized that he couldn't leave her behind. If he proposed to her, he would be giving up the only career he knew and taking an enormous risk. And how would she respond?

Duncan Grant and John Maynard Keynes in 1912. They lived together on the ground floor at 38 Brunswick Square, with Adrian on the first floor, Virginia on the second, and Leonard Woolf right at the top.

At first she demurred, but they spent more time together through the spring of 1912, both in London and at Asheham in Sussex, the larger and more appealing successor to Little Talland House. They had found it while out walking together: a remote, romantic Regency house surrounded by downs and peace, and with a rough, sheep-grazed field stretching away in front. 'The grass of the garden and field seemed almost to come up to the sitting rooms and into the windows', Leonard remembered.[27] They both adored it.

In May, after many careful, exploratory conversations and letters, Virginia told Leonard she loved him. They were extremely honest with each other. Virginia was clear that she was not sexually attracted to Leonard, but she could still imagine their marriage as 'a tremendous living thing, always alive, always hot'.[28] Their affection was empathetic and playful as they planned a life of work, conversation, and freedom. They married in St Pancras Town Hall in August 1912 and quickly set up a routine divided between Asheham and their rented rooms in London, a routine which seemed to both of them 'ideal'. Virginia wrote to the friends who had been her confidantes through the years of single life and told them calmly how happy she was. She was not passionate about Leonard, but she was very certain about him. 'It has been worth waiting for', she told her old teacher Janet Case.[29] Not the least of her happiness was this inalienable fact: 'He has written a novel; so have I.'[30]

The novel she had finished, the 'work of imagination' that had taken all these years and cost her much agonized revision, was *The Voyage Out*.[31] The 'voyage' in question was a journey from England to South America, undertaken by twenty-four-year-old Rachel Vinrace, who is escorted by her aunt Helen away from a narrow domestic life in Richmond into an exotic, unknown terrain. The voyage is also (rather predictably) Rachel's personal journey into adult life. Coming up against

49

other people's opinions, she must repeatedly decide for herself what she thinks; and, coming up against male sexuality for the first time, she must try to understand her own desires.

It was not an especially original framework, but in Woolf's hands this material becomes obscure, slippery, abstract, hinting at things that don't quite crystallize, refusing to resolve into any solidly discernible shape. Challengingly, the heroine is extremely hard to know, and often infuriating. Most of the time she is so silent and inconclusive that there is a space at the centre of the book where we might expect the heroine to be. Entailed in this silence is Woolf's furious indictment of the passivity bred in women, but there is no direct channel along which this fury can flow. 'Doesn't it make your blood boil?' Terence asks Rachel, thinking of the unrepresented views of women, but we hear only the uncertain answer Rachel makes in her mind and the few conciliatory remarks she can voice.[32] At the end of the novel she contracts a violent fever and dies, which feels like her final and uncontrollably physical statement of *something*, but there is no saying what. Perhaps, in the tradition of Maggie Tulliver in *The Mill on the Floss*, Rachel Vinrace is a dreamer who has to die; perhaps her illness is her paralysed rejection of marriage. Or perhaps it is the arbitrary death which does sometimes come for travellers, which came for Thoby Stephen in Greece, and which was not at all a judgment on the way he had lived his life. It is one of the most audacious things about Woolf's fiction that not everything has a meaning.

In this first novel Woolf was courting the idea of self-exposure. She was, after all, writing about a woman who leaves behind a claustrophobic home to explore new ways of living, arrives on the verge of marriage, and then falls into a fever that makes her mad. So there was a strange courage in her decision to make Rachel as naive and embarrassing as she is, to write this story about a young woman's profound social and sexual

The Woolfs' Sussex home Asheham House, drawn by Dora Carrington in 1917.

ignorance, knowing it would be read by a group of urbane, experienced friends. There is no easy self-romanticizing in *The Voyage Out*, though the plot offered plenty of room for it. Helen chides Rachel in a way that would be mortifying for most women of twenty-four: "'Oh Rachel,' she cried. 'It's like having a puppy in the house having you with one – a puppy that brings one's underclothes down into the hall.'"[33] So, though Rachel is a radical thinker, despising the middle-class status quo and wanting to ask big questions, she is not the heroic figure of change Woolf might have chosen. Her bold moves with underclothes are not those of the stylish Bloomsbury iconoclast, but of the unknowing family pet.

This novel written with keen self-consciousness is deeply concerned with 'unknowing'. It looks for the value in what is intuitive. If Rachel is 'like a bird half asleep in its nest', as Terence suggests, that is perhaps part of her power.[34] Her final hallucinations are anticipated by a narcotic atmosphere that characterizes many earlier scenes. Figures loom indistinctly; surface detail evaporates to leave only what Rachel sees: blocks of matter with people moving across them as 'patches of light'.[35] There is a visionary quality about this, and such abstract perception will yield in Woolf's later novels moments of startling clarity. Here there is a note of apologetic dreaminess, and more confusion than clarity. But confusion, in *The Voyage Out*, seems a better way to unravel the truth of things than the hard, bright expressions of certainty to which it is constantly being opposed.

To send this novel out into the world was terrifying. This was exacerbated by the fact that the publisher Woolf sent it to was her half-brother Gerald Duckworth. He accepted it, but this proved the beginning and not the end of Virginia Woolf's publication trials. A year into her marriage – a year which seems to have been happy and productive – she had

Leonard and Virginia Woolf at Asheham, 1914. 'He has written a novel; so have I.'

another breakdown, the first of a series between 1913 and 1915 which were the worst of her life. She went into hospital at Twickenham and longed to get out, but when she got out she got worse. At Brunswick Square in the early evening of 9 September 1913 she took an overdose of Veronal. Geoffrey Keynes, Maynard's brother, was a surgeon at St Bartholomew's and drove Leonard fast to the hospital for a stomach pump. Back at Brunswick Square, a team of doctors and nurses worked for hours to save her. That night she could well have died.

She remained very ill all through the following spring. Leonard established and oversaw a quiet routine at Asheham, which Virginia raged against and submitted to by turns. She had the terrible feeling of wasting both their lives. She was 'grateful and repentant', she told her 'dearest Mongoose'.[36] She was immensely sad. There were months of patient convalescence, during which she trained her racing mind to settle on slow, repetitive tasks. She did basic typing for other people, she gardened, and she learned to cook. *The Voyage Out*, so long delayed, was at last published in March 1915. But Virginia's response to the occasion goes unrecorded. Having suffered, just a few weeks before, the onset of a breakdown more severe than anything she had known, Virginia was too ill to have anything to do with it.

4 Making a Mark 1916–1922

'I suppose I am happy merely because it is so pleasant to be well again.'[1] This was in February 1916 after three years of illness. For two awful months Virginia had refused to see Leonard; the nursing costs had used up their savings (they had needed four live-in nurses at times); Leonard himself was exhausted. The forced feeding had added three stone to Virginia's usual weight, though she could now start to have her normal body shape back. She could also start to enjoy Hogarth House in Richmond, the new home she and Leonard had found together in a hopeful reprieve between breakdowns.

Virginia wanted to live in the centre of London, but she accepted that the space and peace of Richmond was probably much better for her precarious state of health. And if she had to live in the suburbs, Hogarth House was an excellent place to settle. It was a smart Georgian brick house, with rows of sash windows, large, wood-panelled rooms, and, at the back, views across the rooftops to Kew Gardens. The train to London was only a short walk away. That spring Virginia rejoiced in the most ordinary aspects of life because she knew what it was like to lose touch with them. Her convalescence was slow and there would be more setbacks, but nothing so violent or protracted. Seizing every moment of vitality, she launched herself back into the world and back into her writing.

Between 1916 and 1922, Woolf completed two novels,

Night and Day and *Jacob's Room*, novels so different that you might not guess they are by the same writer. The first is packed with the material details of its characters' lives and long conversations about complex feelings, all minutely recorded. The second is a series of moments, each sketched with a few acute lines, surrounded by gaps and ellipses. It is an experimental biography of a young man, and an elegy for him. *Jacob's Room* established a new form for fiction, but it did not come out of nowhere: busy years of reading, writing, and living went into its making.

At first Woolf's work on *Night and Day* was painfully slow. She was allowed to write for an hour in bed each day, and with a novel so solidly realized as this one, an hour did not go very far. She designed it purposely as a steadying, therapeutic book – in both content and form. There were to be no fevers or hallucinations like Rachel's in *The Voyage Out*. This was not a tragedy but a comedy. It was again about a young woman choosing her destiny, but this time all would go well. And in its technical conservatism it was meant to keep Woolf well out of danger. Each character is carefully established against a background before joining the novel's slow dance of pairings and triangles.

Later Woolf talked about *Night and Day* as her 'exercise in the conventional style', as if it were the grammar lesson that would allow her to break the rules in future.[2] Certainly she was dealing in literary conventions (and manipulating them as knowingly as ever Jane Austen did when she married off her heroes just in time for the end). But there were things in this book that had nothing to do with 'exercise'. Virginia Woolf had been exercising as a writer since the age of six. At thirty-four, with all her ambitions yet to be accomplished, she needed to get on with the main performance. *Night and Day* was part of it.

It deals with the question of 'how to live', the question Woolf had discussed so intently with her siblings as they set up their homes and which she still kept asking herself. Her heroine Katharine Hilbery is a young woman of twenty-seven gradually emerging from the shadow of her grandfather's literary genius. She is on the verge of leaving the old Victorian house full of relics and memories, but what power does she have to choose a future? All her ideas about life converge on the one central question of who to marry, so that the traditional courtship plot is also an elaborate, sensualized debate about how to be free.

The relationship between Katharine and Ralph Denham gleams with a sense of something new approaching. Chairs and tables are suddenly not so stable as once they seemed: 'they were solid, for he grasped the back of the chair in which Katharine had sat; and yet they were unreal; the atmosphere was that of a dream'.[3] The apparently unbending framework of English middle-class life looks more malleable when they face it together. The novel is drawn to moments of immanence, pausing on the thresholds of houses, or in the dusk just before the lights come on. And it is full of strange, uncertain things that have no place in the 'conventional style': runaway thoughts, inexplicable symbols, doodles on blotting paper that come unbidden and refuse precise interpretation. And then, near the close, the whole sprawling book is condensed into one simple yet visionary image as powerful as anything Woolf wrote. Katharine is walking with Ralph through the lamplit streets: 'it seemed to her that the immense riddle was answered; the problem had been solved; she held in her hands for one brief moment the globe which we spend our lives in trying to shape, round, whole, and entire from the confusion of chaos'.[4] It is the glimpse of clarity towards which all Woolf's novels strive.

But Woolf does not end with that contained globe. She ends instead with a tribute to the life Katharine has rejected, but which, going on steadily in the background, has made her happiness possible. Katharine and Ralph look up together at the light glowing in the window of Mary Datchett's flat – Mary Datchett who is a single, independent, working woman. They decide not to go in and disturb her: Mary has her work to do. She will be writing books and making plans far into the night. The lovers look up at the light, not with pity but with awe. It was part of Virginia Woolf's farewell gesture to Virginia Stephen, though she would never quite leave this image behind. Often in future, as she compared her own hard-working, bare-seeming life with that of Vanessa, she would console herself with the image of 'forging ahead, alone, through the night'.[5]

Night and Day was Woolf's wartime book (and she finished it with the coming of peace in autumn 1918). Sometimes as she wrote she could hear the sound of guns carried on the wind from northern France. The low rumblings of death were faint, distant, difficult to reconcile with any kind of daily life. In *To the Lighthouse* she would announce the battlefield death of Andrew Ramsay in brackets, so that it seems unreal and remote. The remoteness only adds to the shock and senselessness. Woolf has sometimes been criticized for not facing directly enough the great conflicts of her time, but all her post-war novels are concerned with the indirections by which we come to understand our losses.

Woolf's Great War was inseparable from her personal war against illness. When she writes about the darkness of blackout, the vulnerability of huddling in the basement through an air raid, the strangeness of an orderly world turned against itself, the horror of unknowable forces massed against one, she is writing about both public and private experience. In *Mrs Dalloway* she imagines the thoughts of a shell-shocked war veteran, Septimus Warren-Smith, who sits hallucinating in Regent's Park, seeing, wherever he looks, the same recurring images of the trenches. His visions of war are also the hallucinations of madness, and there is no distinguishing between them.

Woolf wrote *Night and Day* in a protracted effort to kill off her own madness (Septimus in the end had to be killed off too) and her war became one of careful measurement and control. She submitted, on the whole, to quietness, rest, and monitored eating. Her writing was rationed in the same way that the butter was rationed. These were years of austerity lived one day at a time, and with anxiety never far away. Leonard was examined for military service and pronounced unfit, which was a relief but also a confirmation of the effect their troubles had had on his health.

The Woolfs stayed mostly at Asheham, trying to be as self-sufficient as they could. It was not for the faint-hearted, what with the daily round of weeding, herding geese, making bread, fending off mice, bats, and squirrels. This practical work and domestic worry brought Virginia closer and closer to Vanessa, who had leased a farmhouse called Charleston just a few miles away across the meadows. Vanessa had set up home with her new partner and fellow painter Duncan Grant, making room for Clive when he wanted to be there, and welcoming other friends to work on the land. The atmosphere at Charleston never ceased to amaze and inspire Virginia. 'Nessa seems to have slipped civilisation off her back, and splashes about entirely nude', she wrote to Violet (who disapproved), and she was proud to describe her sister as 'an old hen wife, among ducks, chicken and children'.[6] Virginia was in love with this idea of raucous family life; she admitted to Vanessa that

Vanessa Bell with Duncan Grant at Asheham, 1912. They painted
together and shared the excitement of the Post-Impressionist exhibitions;
gradually they fell in love and began a partnership which would last the
rest of their lives.

she wept for it. But her own projects with Leonard were quite different.

They had been thinking for some time about buying a small printing press, but it was not until March 1917 that they finally scraped together enough money. They spent hours and hours teaching themselves how to use it; week after week they made mistakes and had to start pages again. But they both loved the sense of productive independence it gave them. Virginia was quickly established as the typesetter because Leonard's hands were too shaky. It was fiddly, tedious work (none of Vanessa's 'splashing'), but she found it satisfying, a practical therapy that led somewhere.

The press led in fact to a whole new autonomy in her writing. She felt exhilarated by the freedom to publish for herself whatever she chose to write, and the exhilaration showed itself in a series of whirling, somersaulting short stories, which spring up from almost nothing and make patterns in the air. What is there to say about an indistinct mark on a wall? 'Everything', comes the answer, as Woolf spins fantasies about how the mark got there. The mark itself scarcely matters (in the end it turns out to be a snail): the important thing is what the mind can do with it.[7] In these short stories Woolf makes her decisive shift from external facts to inner lives. Thoughts become the facts that matter. The narrator of 'An Unwritten Novel', for example, sits opposite a woman on a train and dreams up her biography, inventing all the details of a disappointed, lonely existence that might explain the sadness in her face.[8] And then the same woman meets her son on the platform at Eastbourne and they go off happily together. The narrator does not know her, cannot know her. People cannot be explained from the outside, and all we can do is to keep on guessing.

Clive Bell with Julian, Quentin, and Angelica, painted by Vanessa
Bell. Vanessa married Clive Bell, an art critic, in 1907. They both had
relationships with other people, but they never divorced and Clive had a
room at Charleston where he stayed regularly. They brought up the three
children as their own, though Angelica was the daughter of Duncan Grant.

It is no coincidence that the transitional years in which Woolf found new fictional forms were the years when she established the daily rhythm of writing her diary. Like many people, she had often started with good intentions in January or written travel journals on holiday. But the diary Woolf began in October 1917 carried on for the rest of her life. At first it was terse and factual, but it quickly filled out. Descriptions of people took on lives of their own, sentences doubled and multiplied as if getting free of rationing. For a while she wrote it daily before tea, but this proved problematic: she wanted to write up the people who came *to* tea. So she took up her pen as soon as they had gone.

Woolf did not conceive her diary as a place of guarded privacy: in fact she kept asking Leonard to make contributions, though his own brief, practical diary gives a sense of why a joint book was never going to work. She started to write for her older self, imagining conversations with Virginia Woolf at fifty. And she was fully aware, especially as she became more famous, that her diary might well be read by others. Reading her accounts of meetings with Yeats or T. S. Eliot, for example, one feels her shaping the moment for posterity. There is surprisingly little about the boredoms, humiliations, and terrors of illness. As usual, she bothered to think through the reasons for this: 'I want to appear a success even to myself.'[9] The diary feels so full and expansive that it is tempting to imagine that all her life is here. It is not, but here is the version of life she wanted to remember.

She tried to include those things that didn't seem important but which, with hindsight, might turn out to be 'the diamonds of the dustheap'.[10] This was closely connected to the development of her fictional writing, where she was feeling for the significance of unremarkable things, knowing that emotion accrues in places you might not at first suspect. Like her fiction,

Woolf's diary was one of her ways of countering life's transience. The thought of days slipping by unrecorded left her with a sense of loss. She hated to think of 'life allowed to waste like a tap left running'.[11]

Some of what she wanted to record was not outwardly eventful at all. Her happiest days were often the quietest. She and Leonard took great joy in a well-organized day that is productive because each activity has its allotted space. Generally they would both work from ten until one: this was the inviolable time when Virginia did her writing, going to her room every morning straight after breakfast, perhaps 'tuning up' with a cigarette and trying out the first words. After lunch she would usually go for a walk, thinking over the morning's writing as she went. Later there would be printing or reading manuscripts, often a visitor for tea. And the evening was the time for that deep, absorbed reading of history and literature that made her ready for the next day's writing. One routine Thursday in 1922, Virginia observed that the day had been 'like a perfect piece of cabinet making – beautifully fitted with beautiful compartments'.[12] It was, to her, profoundly satisfying.

These ordered days belonged mostly to the weeks spent in the country, away from all the interruptions of London. It was a blow when the Woolfs were given six months' notice by their landlord that they would have to leave Asheham. But at an auction in July 1919 they bid in great excitement for a weather-boarded cottage on the very edge of Rodmell village, not far away. It was bought (for £700), and they trundled their furniture across from Asheham in two horse-drawn carts. 'Monk's House', wrote Virginia with satisfaction. 'That will be our address for ever and ever; indeed I've already marked out our graves in the yard which joins our meadow.'[13] It was not morbidity which made her say this: it was a deep sense of peace, continuity, and possession. When they first married, she and Leonard had wanted to be nomadic, but their love of their London and Sussex houses became one of the defining facts of their lives. They found the freedom of nomads in other ways, but they were not wanderers. Their Sussex home, its big garden, and the countryside around it rooted them always.

It was a luxury to have town and country houses, of course, but Monk's House was not luxurious. Rainwater washed from the garden through the house and out of the kitchen door. Nights were frequently disturbed by mice jumping into – or out of – the beds. Potential visitors were warned about the primitive conditions: it wasn't easy to imagine stately Ottoline Morrell, for instance, going to the earth closet in the garden. The gradual improvements at Rodmell, each paid for with the earnings from some particular piece of work, were a continuing source of pride. They had the kitchen redone. They made a writing lodge in the garden. And Virginia's joy in the country was unwavering. In the afternoons she would 'walk out over the flats' thinking over the morning's work, watching the light change on the green slopes of the Downs. She wanted to hold it close and write it down. 'I am so anxious to keep every scrap, you see.'[14]

So the 'tap of life' went streaming into Woolf's diary and into her letters. Often she wrote up the same event in letters for three different people and then for the diary, but rarely is a single phrase repeated. The stream often glittered with gossip, which Woolf treated as a kind of precious currency to be banked and wisely spent. A good piece should elicit something similarly good in return. 'I always keep a sort of pouch of gossip for you in my mind', she told Vanessa, and the pouch got very full.[15]

Much of it was about the friends who congregated at the 1917 Club in London, named for the Russian Revolution. There were afternoons when the older people sat at one end of the room listening in on the gossip of the young. Woolf was now on the 'older' side and feeling, as she got near forty, distinctly middle-aged. She sized up the young people, with their trousers and cropped hair, in ways that were alternately generous and critical. Barbara Hiles, for example, looked bright and modern and ready to get going. But going on what exactly? Woolf was a little sceptical: 'action there is none'.[16] Sometimes the generations fell in love across the gap. Woolf got very caught up in Saxon Sydney-Turner's doomed affair with Barbara; and everyone was embroiled in the strained dynamics between Lytton Strachey, Dora Carrington, and the young Ralph Partridge. Woolf liked to see how other people, other generations, decided to do things. Watching Vanessa's children, she wondered what kind of society they would build. As she talked to Julian she felt she was handing over 'the old things to the new brains'.[17]

While she looked to the future, she remained loyal to old allegiances. Her intimacy with Violet Dickinson had long run its course, but they never stopped corresponding and Virginia never forgot what Violet had done for her. 'It was certainly your doing that I ever survived to write at all', she replied tenderly when Violet praised *Night and Day*.[18] She had survived and she had changed. Whenever Woolf thought about her past – which was often and intensely – she paused to assess how far she had come. What had she to show for her forty years? She was always storing up their riches so that she could be ready with the answer. Going down to Cornwall in the spring of 1921, she felt herself returning to the place from which she had set out: 'I go back "bringing my sheaves".'[19]

She was aware that she was now admired and followed. With two novels out, another one on its way, an American publisher, a growing readership, and fifteen years' worth of regular reviewing behind her, Virginia Woolf was a significant force.

Woolf joked about Ottoline Morrell, but also admired her and valued their friendship.

Mark Gertler, *The Pond at Garsington*, 1916.

Leonard's career too was flourishing: he was busier than ever with editing, lecturing, and politics. Between them they had established a fulfilling way of life. Woolf laughingly imagined herself and Leonard as flowers around which all their buzzing friends would cluster: 'our seductive sweetness appears still to be drawing bees from all quarters'.[20] For both of them, middle age had its rewards. Virginia felt she could at last stride into a milliner's shop, meet the assistant's eye, and get what she wanted. There were plenty of grand nights out: the ballet followed by a party with the Sitwells perhaps, or a weekend at Garsington, with Ottoline 'precisely like the Spanish Armada in full sail'.[21] Virginia liked the feeling of being at the centre of things. 'At a party now I feel a little famous', she noted.[22] People knew her name.

Part of this getting older was the enjoyment of shared memories, hence the founding of a Memoir Club where friends gathered to hear accounts of one another's pasts. There would be dinner and conversation before one or two members stepped up to read a memoir specially composed for the pleasure of the rest. The note of nostalgia linked these friends back to their Victorian parents, who had been so inclined to reminiscence. But the Memoir Club was thoroughly modern in its retrospect, as far from the *Mausoleum Book* as could be. Scandal and laughter set the tone; risqué revelations were always the toast of the evening. Around the table were the people Woolf had first met in Thoby's rooms, and who had been her most lasting and loyal friends.

Her fondness for Saxon Sydney-Turner and Lytton Strachey was always connected with her love for Thoby, but also grew of its own accord. Woolf treated Saxon gently, wanting to be his confidante and waiting patiently for him to say what he meant. With Lytton there was more competition and flair. He was a literary rival: his *Eminent Victorians* had made him a household name in 1918, long before people had heard of Virginia Woolf. And the rivalry spurred them both on. When Lytton dedicated his biography of Queen Victoria to Virginia she was delighted, but she wanted to match his success. Her own short stories, when they came out in 1921, seemed a 'damp firework' next to the sensational sparkling of Strachey: they didn't quite take off.[23] Posterity (for now, at least) has taken a different view of the firework display. *Queen Victoria* looks elegant and accomplished; Virginia Woolf's short stories look to have opened a new chapter in the history of literature.

Lytton was not the only writer with whom she was competing. As she worked on *Jacob's Room*, the book that grew out of her experimental stories, Woolf felt newly aware of her literary contemporaries. She had formed a prickly, awkward, intense friendship with Katherine Mansfield, whose short stories had challenged Woolf to be all the more ambitious in her own. She set the type for Mansfield's long story *Prelude*, one of the earliest publications from the Hogarth Press. 'My God I love to think of you, Virginia, as my friend', wrote Mansfield, offering herself up in a rare moment of self-surrender, wanting to give Woolf 'the freedom of the city without any reserve at all'.[24] But the relationship would be full of reserve, defensiveness, offences given and inferred. Mansfield lashed out with criticism, giving *Night and Day* a cold review. They felt they were working for the same things, but that made them all the more guarded with each other. Their battle had a haunting intimacy about it. When they talked, Woolf had 'the queerest sense of echo coming back to me from her mind the second after I've spoken'.[25]

T. S. Eliot started to visit, but he remained 'Mr Eliot' and it took a long time for the two writers to relax together. Though Woolf wanted them to become friends, it was a delicate

Virginia Woolf with her niece Angelica Bell.

operation. 'What happens with friendships undertaken at the age of 40?' she wondered.[26] She felt slighted by him and not taken seriously when (especially as she was the elder and more established writer) it should have been the other way round. But under the aloofness they were allying themselves. Woolf went to enormous trouble to raise the money that would allow Eliot to leave his bank job. And they started to use the word 'we' when they talked about their writing. 'We're not as good as Keats', Woolf said to him in the back of a taxi to Hammersmith. 'Yes we are', he replied.[27] The following June, Eliot read *The Waste Land* to them at Hogarth House. 'He sang it & chanted it rhythmed it', Virginia recorded, not sure of its meaning as yet but feeling its obscure power beginning to work upon her.[28]

More challenging even than this was the way Eliot talked about James Joyce as the great writer of their age. Woolf couldn't see it. She read *Ulysses* carefully as it came out in instalments, and she acknowledged its technical achievement. But it seemed to her full of stunts and show-off vulgarity. *Ulysses* was much concerned with bodies, but it did not move her sensually. Joyce gave her none of the 'physical pleasure' that she got from reading Proust, and indeed the contrast between her reading of Joyce and Proust in the early 1920s helped to shape her own evolving sense of what she wanted to do. Proust could rouse her every nerve, achieving an 'astonishing vibration and saturation and intensification': 'O if I could write like that!'[29] Her response to *Ulysses* was physical in a different way. Notoriously, she likened its author to a 'queasy undergraduate scratching his pimples'.[30] The image seeped out from her most angry feelings about the exclusivities and irrelevancies of the male educational establishment; *Ulysses* was connected for her with a world of male arrogance and aggressive sexuality. More importantly she found little rhythm or beauty in Joyce's language. Nevertheless, she knew he mattered. When she got stuck with *Jacob's Room* she admitted to herself that 'what I'm doing is probably being better done by Mr Joyce'.[31] It is perhaps revealing that, while she paused, she thought through an article on 'Women', as if needing to rally her forces against these very powerful men.[32]

She had a firm sense of purpose, but Woolf still imagined life as a narrow pavement over an abyss. She had to walk along it without falling in. When life was good, the pavement was wider. There was less chance of falling, but the abyss was always there. A visit from Vanessa – all life and talk and children – could leave her, alone at her writing desk, in tears. Her health during 1921 was precarious and, as was now usual for her, the prospect of publishing a novel made it worse. Each month the doctors came up with a different diagnosis, so she went from having influenza to heart disease to tuberculosis. She had three teeth extracted and the 'microbes' from their roots injected into her arm. Nobody knew (and we cannot now say with any certainty) what was really wrong. She felt, justifiably, that she had lost in total at least five years to the limbo of her illnesses. The tap of life had been running on and she had not been part of it. 'You must call me 35 – not 40 – and expect rather less from me' she instructed E. M. Forster just before her birthday.[33] But her tally was extraordinary for forty, let alone thirty-five. She finished her novel in November 1921, and saw it through to publication, on her own press, in October 1922. It is one of literary history's magical dates, 1922. It was the year of *The Waste Land* and of *Ulysses'* publication in book form – and of *Jacob's Room*.

Woolf's novel began with its hero out of sight; 'Ja-cob! Ja-cob!' shouts his brother, running across the beach in search of him.[34] We do find him – briefly – but all through the novel, as Jacob grows up, goes to university, and falls in love, he keeps eluding the narrator who tries to tell his story. There can be no

73

E. M. Forster by Roger Fry. Forster and Woolf were friends for thirty years, and though Woolf expressed reservations about Forster's writing, she cared a great deal what he thought of hers.

steady, definitive portrait of Jacob, but we glimpse him through the crowd or in a queue, and we hear people talking about him. Like the woman on the train in 'An Unwritten Novel', he is studied and made up by other people. In another very funny and moving train scene, Jacob climbs in opposite old Mrs Norman, who looks round anxiously for the communication cord because 'it is a fact that men are dangerous'; as she 'reads' the appearance of this young man, however, she finds he is 'grave, unconscious', perhaps a little like her own son, someone she wants to talk with – but he gets out at Cambridge and goes on his way.[35]

Jacob's Room fills up with these little shards of experience, but it remains a ghostly book in which a pre-war world is evoked by a detached, lyric voice which seems half to know that it is singing a eulogy. Cheerful bustling sounds keep dying away to silence. The clatter of plates and the hum of talk comes through the night air as dinner is served in Cambridge, but Jacob's room meanwhile is empty and the iron gates in the moonlight are 'lace upon pale green'.[36] When night falls over London, the dome of the British Museum lies pale and still 'as bone lies cool over the visions and heat of the brain'.[37] In Greece, where Jacob goes on his travels, 'darkness drops like a knife'.[38] His mother, in England, thinks she hears the sound of guns. In the next chapter she is holding a pair of her dead son's shoes.

With *Jacob's Room* Woolf felt she had got close to what she wanted to say. It was only an experiment, she kept telling people, an experiment that opened the way for what came next. She was already hard at work on the new novel, pushing on towards a new form. As she pushed forward she also wanted to hold still in the present: '[I] am really very busy, very happy, & only want to say Time, stand still here.'[39]

5 'Drawn on and on'   1923–1925

At Christmas 1922 Woolf wrote a long, reflective letter to her friend Gerald Brenan in Spain, looking back on the year, taking stock, and trying to express what was now driving her onwards. Such moments of summing up, often coming at the end of a year or before the publication of a new book, were important to her. She wanted her life to have form in the way that her novels had form. Now, at the end of 1922, she could feel herself being tugged in different directions and making the choices that would determine who she was in middle age. 'I was wondering to myself why it is that though I try sometimes to limit myself to the thing I do well, I am always drawn on and on, by human beings, I think, out of the little circle of safety, on and on, to the whirlpools; when I go under.'[1] She had worked hard and established herself; she had a successful, devoted husband, a great many friends, and a large house in Richmond. The 'little circle of safety' had about it a magical coherence that she would never stop describing; and yet through the next ten years she would keep going out beyond it. She wrote very quickly, one after the next, four major novels, each completely different from the last, each taking a huge gamble by adopting untried methods. She made new friends and fell in love. She got into the whirlpools, went under, and survived to do it all again.

The most immediate and practical result of Woolf's determination to go beyond safe limits was her conviction that she

Vanessa Bell, *A Conversation (Three Women)*, 1913–16. 'Not a word sounds and yet the room is full of conversations' wrote Virginia Woolf, introducing an exhibition of her sister's paintings in 1934.

and Leonard must move back into central London. Leonard
was against it: Richmond was meant to be good for Virginia's
health. He imagined what would happen if they lived in the
middle of things: late dinners, hundreds of visitors, exhaustion, illness – the dangerous spiral they had known before.
For himself, he loved Hogarth House and felt no great need
of nightly parties. As he dug his heels in, Virginia felt more
trapped. She began to conceive this as a battle for *life*. She had
a painful sense of waste: a sense that if she couldn't get back
to London after nine years in the suburbs, life would irrevoca-
bly pass her by. She wanted to go 'adventuring among human
beings' and was 'inclined for a plunge'.[2] In the novel she was
writing, she went on that adventure, and she thought out the
relationship between the ecstasy of it and the danger. Clarissa
Dalloway walks out into the streets of London one bright
morning and though she is only going to the flower shop, and
though she knows the way by heart, she thrills to the excitement of 'life; London; this moment of June'.[3]

    Mrs Dalloway is about a society woman giving a party –
a strange subject, perhaps, for someone who dreaded smart
society parties. In writing Clarissa, Woolf was thinking partly of
the Stephens' family friend Kitty Maxse, who had symbolized
in youth what it meant to be a social success. Kitty had seemed
grand and imperturbable, and coolly distanced herself from the
Stephen girls when they went off to shabby Bloomsbury. But
then in 1922, unaccountably, perhaps purposely, she fell over
her banisters and died. The image of her returned very powerfully to Woolf: 'her white hair – pink cheeks – how she sat
upright – her voice'.[4] Woolf was at that point writing a series of
stories about Mrs Dalloway, but a few days after Kitty's death
she found that the stories were turning into a novel.

    Woolf worried about her central character. She faltered
and almost abandoned the book when Clarissa seemed 'too

stiff, too glittering & tinsely'.[5] The problem was solved when she found a way to dig what she called 'tunnels' back behind the surface, leading into memories and underground caves of feeling.[6] Woolf still disliked her a little, but she nevertheless gave Clarissa – who was so different from herself – her own feelings about moulding the world, for a moment, to a meaningful design. In Clarissa's house, where things are so cushioned and civilized, all the mixed and violent things of life had somehow to be suggested. She laid out the challenge in a letter to Brenan: 'how does one make people talk about everything in the whole of life, so that one's hair stands on end, in a drawing room?'[7]

Though Woolf's own art form was writing and not the hosting of people in drawing rooms, she generally wanted to be at the centre of the crowd. If she wasn't there she invented it (as she did with resigned good humour when she missed one of her own parties in 1925), thereby eliminating all risk of disappointment: 'I lay in bed and imagined it. Never shall I go to a party in any other way. One is so brilliant; so happy; so beautiful.'[8] She loved the gossip and the web of human relations. She loved the element of disguise involved, whether it was putting on a flirtatious social manner or cross-dressing for one of Duncan Grant's risqué ballets. Dramatic conversation was part of the performance.

Woolf liked her power to intimidate people, and her power to inspire them. She even liked the occasional sign that she was herself in danger of becoming fashionable. She took advice on make-up from Clive's partner, the showy Mary Hutchinson (together they were called in Woolf's private zoo-language 'the parakeets'); Dorothy Todd, the editor of *Vogue*, wanted to take her shopping; the dauntless Sibyl Colefax wanted her at the table. But it was the old foundations beneath it all that moved her most. Woolf marvelled at the invisible ties that kept bringing her old friends back together, however different and distant the lives they now led. Waking up after a party to have breakfast on a grey morning with the Bells and the Partridges, she had a profound sense of belonging to a community. It seemed that 'Bloomsbury' after all, had meant something. 'If six people, with no special start except what their wits give them, can so dominate, there must be some reason in it', she wrote to Gwen Raverat. 'Where they seem to me to triumph is in having worked out a view of life […] which still holds, and keeps them dining together, and staying together, after 20 years.'9 It is a remark that points forward to *The Waves*, the novel in which she drew on these deep feelings for the circle of much-loved people in whose company she chose to live.

By the autumn of 1923 Virginia had won her battle for London, and after some excited house-hunting, she and Leonard took a ten-year lease on 52 Tavistock Square. It was an 1820s town house on five floors, with the ground and first floors already let to a firm of solicitors. So the Woolfs arranged two separate but connecting spaces. Down in the basement there was a maze of rooms for the ever-expanding Hogarth Press, leading to a former billiards room at the back which Virginia took as her study. She worked in a dishevelled armchair, surrounded by piles of Hogarth manuscripts among which, every so often, an apprehensive editorial assistant would come foraging while trying not to disturb the hunched figure by the gas fire with the writing board on her knees. In the basement it was all industry, but upstairs, on the second and third floors, the reception rooms were decorated with painted panels by Grant and Bell, the armchairs were in a better state, and from the windows there was a view towards the 'pale tower' of St Pancras Church.

Virginia was immediately writing odes to London, wondering at her own romanticism. Even the moon looked more like the real thing here than in Richmond. She felt she had stored up a whole decade of talking that would now be released, night after night, with her friends around her fire. Tavistock Square was right in the middle of her old territory, with Gordon Square just next door and the probability of bumping into people she knew whenever she left the house. She could dip into the outdoor world at any moment and then return to work.

She was back, and the time away from London now seemed merely an interruption. She felt as if she were 'going on with a story' that had been started in 1904, when the Stephens moved out of Hyde Park Gate.[10] Her past now felt very close, so that any odd sound could set off memories. Just the squeak of a door hinge takes Clarissa Dalloway back to the house of her youth, where the doors were flung open and the same feeling of starting out fills her all over again: 'What a lark, what a plunge!'[11]

There was something else that made Woolf feel young again in the spring of 1924, and filled her with anticipation. Among those who increasingly came to visit was an aristocratic writer of thirty, admiring her novels and exuding patrician style. Vita Sackville-West seemed to stride expansively through the world. She brought with her the spirit of Knole, the great house in which she had grown up; and in her trail came stories of elopement with the cross-dressing Violet Trefusis. And here she was on Virginia's doorstep.

The life of Bloomsbury, with its serious talk, its scorn of glitter, its 'slippers, smoke, buns, chocolate', was very different from what Vita was used to. She would later call it 'Gloomsbury'.[12] When she went down to Rodmell her very presence made Monk's House look like a 'ruined barn'.[13] But there was no mistaking the fact that Vita was paying court to Virginia Woolf. She finished a novel for the Hogarth Press and

THE HOGARTH PRESS

52 TAVISTOCK SQUARE, LONDON, W.C.1.

AUTUMN ANNOUNCEMENTS

1924

The Hogarth Press autumn announcements of 1924, with a drawing by
Vanessa Bell. The Woolfs were professional publishers running an admired
and influential business. That year saw Hogarth issuing the first two
volumes of *Collected Papers* by Sigmund Freud, Virginia Woolf's *Mr Bennett
and Mrs Brown* for the Hogarth Essays, and Vita Sackville-West's *Seducers
in Ecuador*.

dedicated it to Virginia, who was seized with 'childlike dazzled affection' when she found her name on the flyleaf under the exotic title *Seducers in Ecuador*.[14]

This growing mid-life relationship began to make Woolf too feel exotic. She immediately made capital out of it with her sister, dropping casual erotic references into her letters after years in the shadow of Vanessa's sexual adventurousness. Fantasizing to her friends about Vita as the embodiment of all English history 'from 1300 to the present day', she teasingly slipped between fiction and seriousness in a way that gave her licence to say anything at all.[15] 'To tell you a secret,' she wrote to Jacques Raverat in France, 'I want to incite my lady to elope with me next.'[16] She was going to do no such thing, except in imagination and language; her attachment to her old friends and above all to her life with Leonard was unshakeable. But 'Oh yes, I do like her', she wrote in her diary one evening in September as she simultaneously looked forward to Leonard's return from work, hoping every minute that he would appear, and watching their dog Grizzle prick up his ears hopefully at any approaching sound.[17]

Woolf's new confidence buoyed up her novel, which had to be confident. Choosing to follow characters through a city on one day in June, she was explicitly mounting her riposte to *Ulysses*. And even as she did this she was setting – letter by letter – the type for the Hogarth Press edition of *The Waste Land*. She needed to respond to the challenge of her contemporaries, and at the same time she wanted to consolidate her reputation as a critic – not just a journalist now, but an essayist with a distinctive voice. She collected some of her longer review articles and started to 'refurbish' them for publication in a book she called 'Reading' and which became *The Common Reader*. The bits and pieces of her critical work were now to form some kind of whole, a sustained exploration of what literature can do.

Already Woolf had plenty of material for this book, but to keep herself fresh, and because she was alive with energy, she embarked on formidably ambitious new essays. Two years' worth of reading Homer, Aeschylus, Euripides, and Sophocles went into a piece called 'On Not Knowing Greek'. The title sounded like a defensive reference to Woolf's lack of formal education, but this was a purposeful red herring. The classics don and the common reader were in the same boat since neither *really* knew Greek and neither was there in the theatre at Athens. It is imagination more than scholarship that will take the reader back into that world.

The Common Reader moves easily from Chaucer's bare, chilly, muddy medieval England to the polished surface of Addison's prose; from lives of the great to 'Lives of the Obscure'.[18] Woolf conjures a background for her subjects, evoking a particular texture and temperature of life, taking us close to the writing of the past, but at the same time exposing the gaps and doubts that show us how far away we are. In each essay, Woolf's attempt to convey the character of literature is like her attempt to convey character in fiction. 'How did she differ?' Lily Briscoe will ask about Mrs Ramsay in *To the Lighthouse*: 'What was the spirit in her, the essential thing, by which, had you found a glove in the corner of a sofa, you would have known it, by its twisted finger, hers indisputably?'[19] This is what Woolf wants to know about every book she opens. If you found a few pages of Tolstoy, or Defoe, or Euripides on the sofa, how would you know the writing to be theirs, indisputably?

For much of the time she was working on *The Common Reader* and *Mrs Dalloway*, Woolf felt more intensely happy than ever before, but she felt the fragility of this happiness. The disorientating highs and lows of January 1923 seemed to set a rhythm. The year began with a Twelfth Night party at Gordon Square, given by Maynard Keynes. By all accounts it was the sort of party of which mythologies are made. There was Lydia Lopokova dancing and Walter Sickert acting Hamlet; everyone seemed glowing and gifted. Virginia felt her blood prickling like champagne with the pleasure of it all. Dressed in her 'mother's laces', she thought of her parents and all that had changed for her generation, and wondered, did their fathers ever enjoy themselves like this?[20] But while Woolf was at the party Katherine Mansfield was dying. The news came mid-month and Woolf immediately felt an emptiness in her writing. 'Katherine won't read it', she thought.[21] She kept seeing an image of Katherine putting on a white wreath.

The pleasures and the pains continued in tandem. Woolf's mind was racing with plans, but she kept being held back by flu and temperatures. She watched, sad and disturbed, as her brother Adrian's marriage fell apart. And beneath everything, despite her success, Woolf still envied her sister's family life and felt – as always – an outsider wheeling beyond that particular circle of light. She kept being aware of life and death as competing forces. On the anniversary of her mother's death she spent a few moments remembering ('how I laughed, for instance, behind the hand which was meant to hide my tears') and then she shut it out, using a phrase from her recent essay on Montaigne: 'enough of death – its life that matters'.[22] She wanted to keep 'pressing forward, thinking, planning, imagining'.[23]

So Virginia Woolf in her early forties felt both at the very centre of things and on the periphery; she was well and buoyant, but aware of illness in the sidelines. She felt old and established, but also very young, as if she were just beginning. She was holding together different versions of herself and those differences gave her the framework for her novel. Woolf knew that the structure of *Mrs Dalloway* was more original than anything she had done so far. It was a design that allowed

Bloomsbury performances: Lydia Lopokova came to London with
Diaghilev's celebrated *Ballets Russes*, danced at parties in Gordon Square,
and married Maynard Keynes in 1925.

Virginia Woolf wearing her mother's dress, photographed by Maurice Beck and Helen Macgregor for *Vogue* in 1924. She wore one of Julia's dresses in higher spirits for a Twelfth Night party in 1923 and wondered whether her parents had ever enjoyed themselves like this.

for incongruous things to go along side by side. There is Clarissa Dalloway, going through her day and having her party. And there is also Septimus Warren-Smith, a war veteran, in London on the same day and haunted by visions of the trenches.

In writing Septimus, Woolf was imaginatively re-entering her own experiences of illness. This was exactly what she had needed to avoid while writing *Night and Day*, but now she felt able to do it. There were times when her work on 'the mad part' was extremely disturbing, as when she went out in the rain one evening in the hope of meeting Leonard from the train. Not finding him, she was overcome by loneliness and felt her battle with the 'old devil' rising up. When Leonard finally appeared in his mackintosh, talking about his day at the office, her relief was ecstatic. She was safe, and yet 'there was something terrible behind it'.[24] A year later, in October 1924, she could congratulate herself on finishing the book in good health. It was a triumph over the illness she had been writing about.

Clarissa and Septimus do not know each other and they do not meet. Their lives are linked by being alive at the same time in the same city, looking up at the same aeroplane and feeling the same sunshine. The novel is a diptych, and though the panels are not hinged by anything solid or definable, invisible lines run between them. Leading their separate lives, Clarissa and Septimus are held together by the design of the novel. This was a high-risk strategy. Another writer would have brought them into contact: they might be long-lost cousins, or at the very least they would have a conversation. Woolf refuses those easy options. In the middle of the party Clarissa hears that a young man has killed himself. She vividly imagines his death and then, in a kind of resurrection, she goes back to her guests. They see her standing there: 'for there she was'.[25] This book about the strangely entwined fates of two

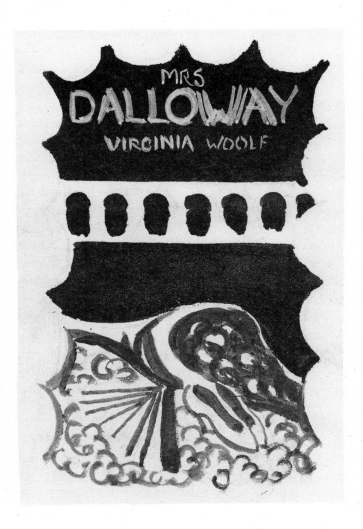

Vanessa Bell's jacket design for her sister's fourth novel *Mrs Dalloway*.

people bears the name of only one of them and it is she, the survivor, who stands there at the end.

While she was revising *Mrs Dalloway*, Woolf was writing long, warm letters to her old friend the painter Jacques Raverat. He was living in France with his wife, the engraver Gwen Raverat, and he was crippled by multiple sclerosis. Unable to hold a pen, he would dictate to Gwen his letters for Virginia, and in return she would send vivid round-ups of Bloomsbury gossip. She sent him the proofs of her novel, something she did for no one else except Leonard. When Gwen read it aloud to him she edited out the death of Septimus, finding it too upsetting. Woolf wanted to dedicate the book to Jacques, but wasn't able to ask: the news of Jacques's death reached Tavistock Square in March. *The Common Reader* was published in April, followed three weeks later by *Mrs Dalloway* (fulfilling precisely the ambitious timetable Woolf had set herself a year before). She was very much at the party during these months and she was conscious of banishing death in order to keep going. But she kept on writing to Gwen and thinking about Jacques, feeling that it was 'merely a break in the talk',[26] and knowing how very closely the living are connected to the dead.

6 'This is it' 1925–1927

The conversation with the past would not let her go. On her
usual walk round Tavistock Square in the spring of 1925,
Woolf suddenly thought of the shape for a novel. As with
many of her other books, it was the shape which came first
and which endured. She quickly sketched it out in a notebook:
an 'H' shape, 'two blocks joined by a corridor'.[1] There was the
past, and then a break, and then a reconvening. This simple
structure embodied the plot and the point of *To the Lighthouse*.

Woolf acknowledged that this novel was a laying to rest
of ghosts from her family past. 'I wrote the book very quickly',
she said later, 'and when it was written, I ceased to be obsessed
by my mother. I no longer hear her voice; I do not see her.'[2]
She had altered her memories of her father as well: 'now he
comes back sometimes, but differently.'[3] Her process of writing
about these two powerful figures, which she compared to psy-
choanalysis, did not make them any less present in her mind:
she would go back to them later in *The Years* and again in her
memoir 'Sketch of the Past'. But in *To the Lighthouse* she started
to take control of her relationship with them.

She had first to summon them up. In writing Mr and Mrs
Ramsay she was drawing on her memories of her parents and
seeing them through the eyes of a child – eight children in fact,
because the eight Ramsay children, all of different ages, allow
her to track something of what it was like to grow up in that

Julia Jackson (later Julia Stephen) photographed by Julia Margaret
Cameron in 1867.

family. Yet Woolf wanted to see Mr and Mrs Ramsay not only in the passionate, exaggerated, dependent way that a child knows his or her parents, but also in the steady, empathetic way that an adult can come to understand other adults. At the age of forty-four, then, Woolf made a portrait of her parents as they were in middle age, looking at them face to face. When Vanessa read the book she immediately recognized their mother: 'It was like meeting her again with oneself grown up and on equal terms.'[4]

When Woolf looked at her parents she found aspects of herself. She saw things she needed to rebel against and things which, for better or worse, there was no getting away from. So when she laughs at the self-involved Mr Ramsay, who leaps around, arms waving, quoting poetry, seeking truth, she is getting an ironic distance on her father and also on herself. She was not going to write concise lives of national heroes in alphabetical order, nor conceive her intellectual life as a logical progression from A to Z. But Mr Ramsay's obsessive dedication to his work is hers. So are his ambition, his eccentricity, his desire for protection, and the tuning of his life to the quotations always running in his mind.

Her portrait of the Ramsay marriage is also an exploration of her own. The writing of *To the Lighthouse* coincided with the most intense period of her relationship with Vita Sackville-West and the novel took fire from the love affair. But it was separate from Vita ('Oh but you shan't read it. Its a ghost between us.'[5]). It was her long marriage, rather than this recent liaison, which seems most to have coloured Woolf's writing. The presence of Vita brought into focus the contentment of her life with Leonard, and it was at just this time that she paid moving tribute in her diary to their marriage. She defended its 'dailiness', arguing that though much of married life becomes automatic, the 'bead of sensation' that forms here and there is

Leonard Woolf and his spaniel Sally, by Vanessa Bell. In June 1925 Virginia
celebrated in her diary her daily life with Leonard: 'making an ice, opening a
letter, sitting down after dinner, side by side, & saying "Are you in your stall,
brother?" – well what can trouble this happiness?'

exquisite precisely because so much unconsidered shared experience has accrued.[6] She celebrated the small happiness of taking the bus together or opening a letter, or 'sitting down after dinner, side by side, & saying "Are you in your stall, brother?"'[7] This was the background against which she wrote the after-dinner scene where Mr and Mrs Ramsay are at last left alone at the end of the day.

If Woolf is inside the Ramsay marriage, she is more obviously outside it, in the figure of Lily Briscoe, though Lily is in no simple way a portrait of the artist. In early drafts the painter was a minor character, off painting hedgerows. But she became the central orchestrating figure, the woman who is trying to understand herself and her relation to the whole Ramsay family by painting a portrait of Mrs Ramsay and her son sitting on the steps of the house. Woolf might easily have made Lily one of the Ramsay children, a daughter, like herself, of the woman she was painting. But she chose instead a less easily definable standpoint. Lily is a friend, so she is outside the family. She is held in place by a strong but uncertain tie to Mrs Ramsay and her domestic world. There is room to suppose some erotic attraction, and there is a connection with Woolf's feelings for Vita, but Woolf was not going to pin down this relationship. She leaves her artist as a purposely obscure figure whose life we do not know.

Some old anxieties go into this portrait. Lily is childless and extraneous to the busy life of the family. She is sensitive to criticism and perennially dogged by the sense of Mr Ramsay bearing down on her, ready to cast judgment. But it is this same Lily who triumphs. It is she who is able to say, 'I have had my vision.'[8] As she completes her painting she is thinking of Mr Ramsay arriving at the lighthouse; her final brushstroke marks the completion of his journey as well as hers. So it is in the imagination of the artist that everyone is finally brought together and momentarily at peace, as the disparate characters of *The Waves* will survive in the mind of the writer Bernard, given voice by him alone at the close.

Lily's 'vision', when it comes, is very simple. She sees Mrs Ramsay knitting on the step: 'There she sat.'[9] It echoes the reappearance of Clarissa, who has survived death and returned to the party, at the end of *Mrs Dalloway*: 'For there she was.'[10] It is these plain facts that carry the emotional weight in Woolf's writing. She may be in some ways a complicated writer, but she is always reaching for the most irreducible of statements. Lily need only make one final line down the centre of her picture to complete it – but it has to be the right line: 'She looked at the steps; they were empty; she looked at her canvas; it was blurred. With a sudden intensity, as if she saw it clear for a second, she drew a line there, in the centre.'[11]

Woolf was working towards a philosophy about these moments of clarity. She had experienced them all her life, as shocks or revelations, moments in which what was blurred becomes in an instant very clear. Walking through Bloomsbury one night in February 1926 (a year after seeing *To the Lighthouse* suddenly, very clearly, in Tavistock Square), she looked at the night sky, thinking of the same moon over Vita in Persia, and she had a 'great & astonishing sense of something there, which is "it"'.[12] In her diary the following day she asked: 'Why is there not a discovery in life? Something one can lay hands on & say "This is it?"'[13]

The question sounded all through the novel she was writing, and resolved itself into the extraordinary affirmation of Lily's vision at the end. But Virginia Woolf did not believe in a god, and if she sensed 'something there' it had nothing to do with Christianity. Her devout atheism was part of the inheritance she was writing about. Both her parents had been through a painful loss of faith and had worked strenuously

Leslie Stephen, 1900. In May 1927, Woolf explained to Vita the difficulty of writing about her father in *To the Lighthouse*. 'I was more like him than her, I think; and therefore more critical: but he was an adorable man, and somehow, tremendous.'

towards a rationalist philosophy to replace it. Mr Ramsay, arriving at the lighthouse, stands up straight in the bow of the boat, 'for all the world, James thought, as if he were saying "There is no God"'. [14] He seems to James rather ridiculous, but the scene is not entirely emptied of heroism. It is part of a powerful religious current in a novel which insistently borrows Christian iconography and puts it at the service of daily secular life. The dinner party scene is a ceremonial last supper, and the journey to the lighthouse is a necessary pilgrimage. Lily's picture is in the long tradition of Madonna and Child paintings, but it is Mrs Ramsay and her son James, not the Holy Family, who are sacred to her.

Fifteen years later, when she was making notes for an autobiography and trying to articulate her need to write, Woolf arrived at something she was willing to call 'a philosophy':

> that behind the cotton wool is hidden a pattern; that we – I mean all human beings – are connected with this; that the whole world is a work of art. *Hamlet* or a Beethoven quartet is the truth about this vast mass that we call the world. But there is no Shakespeare, there is no Beethoven; certainly and emphatically there is no God; we are the words; we are the music; we are the thing itself.[15]

She had taken on the imagined voice of Mr Ramsay standing up in the boat as he reaches the lighthouse, though here it does not sound ridiculous at all.

7   A Writer's Holiday   1927–1928

To many of Virginia Woolf's literary admirers, the appearance of *Orlando* in 1928, a year after *To the Lighthouse*, was a shock. The whole tone of it was different from her previous novels. The writer Elizabeth Bowen remembered her surprise: 'This *Orlando* – we did not care for the sound of it. The book was, we gathered, in the nature of a prank, or a private joke; worse still, its genesis was personal.' The Virginia Woolf they had previously admired was remote and impersonal. 'We visualised her less as a woman at work than as a light widening as it brightened [...] Seldom can a living artist have been so – literally – idealized.'[1] *Orlando* did not fit.

The abstract idea of Woolf still dominates many readings of her, and for good reason, but part of Woolf's appeal is her tremendous variety. When she finished *To the Lighthouse*, after six months of retyping and 'screwing her brain' to the task of revision, she wanted a break. She wanted to write something quickly and for fun. 'I feel in need of an escapade', she wrote in March 1927, and after a summer of reviewing she was able, in the autumn, to take off.[2] At first she conceived a book about her friends, including Vita as 'Orlando, a nobleman'.[3] Orlando the nobleman quickly took over the whole enterprise, and in October Woolf was writing very fast with 'the greatest rapture'. By March the first draft was finished and she was looking back with satisfaction on 'a writer's holiday'.[4]

From now on Woolf would often have something fun on the go to keep herself afloat. *Flush*, her biography of Elizabeth Barrett Browning's spaniel, would be a rest after *The Waves* and *Between the Acts*, a 'holiday' from writing her life of Roger Fry. But we need not put any of these on a separate shelf. There is plenty of holiday spirit in Woolf's most intensely lyric novels. Look for the author of *Orlando* in *To the Lighthouse* and the dashing social comedy comes leaping into view. It is still perhaps the most underestimated aspect of that much-discussed novel: Mr Ramsay seeing all humanity rayed out among the geranium leaves, or Charles Tansley asking, 'did one like his tie?' – and 'God knows, said Rose, one did not.'[5]

Virginia Woolf's wit was addictive and formidable. Her jokes, like most jokes, had to be quick, and she wanted *Orlando* to be 'written as I write letters at the top of my speed'.[6] The novel was, from the first, connected with the skimming, glittering voice of her correspondence – especially her long, sexy, teasing letters to Vita Sackville-West. Each was a game of close reading, where the words stood in lieu of the body: 'Read between the lines, donkey West; put on your horn spectacles, and the arid ridges of my prose will be seen to flower like the desert in spring: cyclamens, violets, all a growing, all a blowing.'[7] This is the voice that takes us on the wild-goose chase of *Orlando*, beckoning us on through an accumulation of rapid-flowering details, spinning out fantasies with unruffled composure, sub-clause after sub-clause, moving so fast that we can't possibly stop to protest, until at last we reach the end of a paragraph with a flirtatious dot-dot-dot.

The comedy of *Orlando* comes as no surprise to the reader of her letters; and in its themes too it is intricately connected with Woolf's other work. In a tone 'half laughing, half serious', it asks the same enduring questions.[8] How different are men and women? Did our ancestors experience life in the same

Vita Sackville-West posing as 'Orlando about the year 1840'. 'Do you exist?'
Woolf wondered in a letter of March 1928; 'Have I made you up?'

Vanessa Bell's endpapers for *Flush*, Woolf's biography of Elizabeth Barrett
Browning's dog.

ways as us? What do we inherit from our family pasts? That last question links Woolf's project of family history in *To the Lighthouse* with her fantasizing of Sackville-West's ancestors in *Orlando*. Both are books about inheritance, asking how much is set down from the start and how far we are free to invent ourselves. Orlando *is* her ancestors, but she also remakes herself with each passing century.

It is a sign of Woolf's confidence that *Orlando* not only connects with previous novels but makes a public joke of her famous style. There is, for example, a parody of the 'Time Passes' section from *To the Lighthouse*, and in a way the whole book was a riff on the 'flight of time' which her friends had once dared her to write. Woolf was parodying herself in other ways too, caricaturing herself as much as Vita. Orlando is visited by the great poet Nick Greene, who cuts a shabby figure at the dining table, talking about his illnesses, invoking literary glory in a bad French accent, and dismissing all other writers of his generation, who happen to be Shakespeare, Marlowe, and Donne. Woolf (whose spoken French was never a strong point) was thoroughly self-knowing about her dismissal of Joyce. And she knew she had slighted Vita's poetry: poor Orlando can't get a word in edgeways about his own writing, but is so unaccountably enchanted that he goes on listening until Greene gets fed up with rural life and goes back to London where he belongs – and where, dipping his pen into the eggcup that serves for an inkpot, he proceeds to write a satire on his ill-used country host.[9]

Though the book was not the 'outline of her friends' that Woolf first conceived (that idea branched off into *The Waves*), *Orlando* was shaped by her long friendship with Lytton Strachey. For twenty years they had been showing off, outwitting each other, competing for sexual shock value. A gender-changing fantasy stood a good chance of rivalling Strachey's famous openness about 'buggery'; and a 500-year biography might challenge even such a controversial form of life-writing as Strachey had practised in *Eminent Victorians*, where a telling anecdote or two might replace volumes of pious detail. Strachey thought Woolf had chosen the wrong kind of subject matter in her novels and should try something more like *Tristram Shandy*, which is exactly what she did in *Orlando*. She reread Sterne's comic epic in 1926 and borrowed its penchant for mock prefaces and indexes, tantalizing gaps, double entendres, documents scorched in the middle of the most important sentence. Tristram has difficulty getting born; Orlando shows no prospect of dying.

So *Orlando* was an answer to Lytton. But it was first and foremost an extended letter to Vita, designed for the world to read. Woolf began it just as the closest phase of their affair was coming to an end. Vita, though still devoted, saw that Virginia could give no long-term sexual commitment, and was turning to other women for the stable intimacy she wanted. *Orlando* was a kind of consolation to both of them for the fact that they would not go on being lovers; it was also Woolf's way of managing her jealousy, fondly punishing Vita, and paying tribute to what they had had. Since Christmas 1925 there had been days when Vita was 'pink glowing, grape clustered, pearl hung'; she had brought with her into Virginia's life 'the glow & the flattery & the festival'.[10] There had been long periods during Vita's trips abroad when Virginia played the pining lover waiting 'doggedly, dismally, faithfully' for her return, frightened by the strength of her own feeling.[11] They had talked by the fire, and very occasionally they had slept together. 'Twice', Vita said, though this was in a letter to her husband, to whom she swore that her love was more 'spiritual' than sexual.[12] It may well have been the truth: certainly Vita was anxious about making Virginia ill. For her part, Virginia understood this danger well. Both had, at a certain point, held back:

Lytton Strachey, Woolf's great friend, rival, and literary accomplice.
He is painted here by Dora Carrington, with whom he lived at
Tidmarsh Mill and later Ham Spray House.

Talking to Lytton the other night he suddenly asked
me to advise him in love – whether to go on, over the
precipice, or stop short at the top. Stop, stop! I cried,
thinking instantly of you. Now what would happen if
I let myself go over? Answer me that. Over what? you'll
say. A precipice marked V.[13]

There was too much to lose in going over. By the end of
1927 Woolf was safe, and could enjoy the vertigo of the precipice by writing it out in *Orlando*. The novel castigates prudery,
while all the time revelling in concealments more fulsome
than furbelows. Body parts are glimpsed one at a time. Like
the sixteenth-century love poems that praise a mistress's eyes,
mouth, neck, cheek all separately, the narrative eye of *Orlando*
keeps homing in on a hand or a foot. Orlando's legs are men-
tioned unreasonably often. 'A thousand pities that such a pair
of legs should leave the country', sighs Nell Gwyn as Orlando
sets off for Constantinople; and when he becomes a woman
Orlando has to be careful because, should her legs be exposed
for a moment, any passing sailor might be so distracted as to
fall head first from his mast.[14]

Woolf's sensuality, as usual, is not in the strip but the tease.
This was her preference, but it was also a practical tactic, since
it allowed her to publish a lengthy celebration of a lesbian at a
time when the most dully unerotic of lesbian novels (most
notably Radclyffe Hall's *The Well of Loneliness*) were falling prey
to the censors. Through a series of events made by Virginia
Woolf's cunning to look like her hero's pure good luck,
Orlando never actually falls in love with anyone who happens
to be of the same sex: s/he changes in tune with her suitors.

Virginia's sense of Vita as a woman capable of being
many selves at once (wife, mother, lover, man, woman, writer,
gardener, aristocrat, gypsy) was the inspiration for a fictional

shape-shifter who plays out hundreds of roles across the centuries, adapting to different societies, and yet all along being unmistakably herself. The novel rejoices in metamorphoses worthy of Ovid, from the transformations of Orlando herself to the woman from Norwich who turns to dust in the frost. The spirit of Shakespearean comedy is always close to the surface, bringing with it a joyous web of disguises and confusions. In sending Orlando off as Extraordinary Ambassador to Constantinople in the seventeenth century, Woolf was thinking of Vita's time in Persia, where her husband Harold Nicolson was posted as a diplomat. But she was also alluding to an exotic strain in Vita that reached much further back – to her grandmother Pepita, a Spanish dancer of Romani descent.[15] Accordingly, Orlando lives joyously for a time with a group of Gypsies and herds goats on the slopes of Mount Athos.

When Vita went off travelling, Virginia generally stayed in England and wrote letters about the beauty of an English spring. But there was plenty of the roaming spirit in Virginia, and Orlando's adventurous shape-shifting is hers as well. There had been the succession of European trips in her twenties, to Turkey, Greece, Italy. After *Mrs Dalloway* there was a long stay with Brenan in the Sierra Nevada in Spain (reached after days of plodding though the desert on mules); when Vanessa started to spend chunks of the year in the south of France, Leonard and Virginia got into the habit of taking holidays in Cassis, near Marseilles. They went in 1927, 1928, and 1929, enjoying the warmth and the pace of life. Virginia was so taken with it that she started house-hunting, arranged to buy a small villa, and had some furniture shipped over before Leonard managed to persuade her of the impracticalities of owning a house many hundred miles from where they worked. In subsequent years there were adventures with the Frys in Greece and tipsy nights of Chianti in Italy. Woolf's ready fund of metaphors always

Roger Fry, *View of Cassis*, 1925. Vanessa Bell and Duncan Grant built a
house in Cassis and the Woolfs went out to join them for a series of holidays
in the 1920s. Moths flying, frogs croaking, warmth, light, food: Virginia
enjoyed it so much that she almost bought a house there.

took on local colour. After a holiday in Spain writing itself was mere 'tossing of omelettes'.[16] Wherever she was, Woolf pledged her enduring love of it. She wanted to catch every new sight and sensation in words. Rattling along on the train home from Greece, she was still writing, writing, writing until her eyes were sore. She would never be at home abroad in the way that both Vanessa and Vita were, but the sun brought out in her a whole new stream of fantasies.

In late October 1928, just after the publication of *Orlando*, Woolf gave the much-mythologized lectures at Cambridge which developed into her book-length essay *A Room of One's Own*. It is one of the most celebrated and controversial discussions of women's liberty, and its power comes largely from its methods of suggestion and indirection. The style owed much to the mischievous methods of her holiday novel: doodling, humming, eating and drinking, whisking up an imagined biography of Shakespeare's sister. But it is also about what it says it's about: the need for a woman to have money and a room of her own. Woolf argues quite plainly for the importance of those material comforts which allow a woman to concentrate her energies in her intellectual life (since it is hard to write poetry when you are cold, or interrupted, or need to make a pie). She also argues unashamedly for the pleasure of material comforts per se. Why shouldn't a woman have a decent dinner and a good chair to sit in? she asks, contrasting the meagre prunes at a women's college with the splendid food that the men enjoyed just down the road.

Her own capacity to make money was a deep source of satisfaction, and she wanted to translate her money into life-enhancing *things*. She never stopped wondering at the alchemy by which the products of her imagination turned into vases or chairs: *Mrs Dalloway* bought a bathroom at Monk's House and

Sissinghurst Castle in Kent, the home of Harold Nicolson and Vita Sackville-West from 1930.

two WCs (one of which was called Mrs Dalloway's Lavatory); *To the Lighthouse* bought a car. Like the excellent lunch in *A Room of One's Own*, the car encourages the expansiveness of mind that might result in good writing. We can feel the effects of the Woolfs' Singer car (called The Lighthouse) in the pages of *Orlando*. Scenes flash by, the world opens up. Virginia never mastered the art of driving, despite lessons with Vita in Kensington Gardens; after a few hair-raising outings Leonard firmly took the wheel. But the car made Virginia feel freer than ever before. Next, with the proceeds of *Orlando*, she had a new bedroom built for herself at Monk's House: the room of one's own in which to write and dream.

The idea of literary inheritance in *A Room of One's Own* is like the continuity of bloodlines in *Orlando*. Just as Orlando in the present day holds within her all the experiences of her Renaissance self, so Virginia Woolf *is* also Shakespeare's sister, carrying on the same work, building on the foundations laid by that obscure woman whose world would not let her write. Woolf's response in *A Room of One's Own* to her literary forebears is her autobiography as much as her family memoir is her autobiography. For all her competitiveness, Woolf felt profoundly a sense of shared endeavour and familial connection. 'Books continue each other,' she says, 'in spite of our habit of judging them separately.'[17]

Her next book would itself continue the work of *Orlando* and *A Room of One's Own*, though it looked very different. In the 'mystic', serious, exploratory novel she wrote between 1929 and 1931 she thought again about the many roles played by each individual, and the many people who make each of us what we are. It was the 'outline of all my friends' she had started to write earlier and which had been usurped by Vita alone.[18] Now she imagined the lives of friends as so interwoven that they 'continue each other'.

8   Voices   1929–1932

The Waves is a book of voices. Six characters speak in turn, three men and three women, each articulating his or her own pleasures and fears, each responding to the other five, working out how they are different and how they are the same. They play together as children in the same garden, and then the boys go away to school, university, and work, while the girls make their lives at home. They have families; they part; they come together. They get older, they compete with one another, they go their separate ways, and yet still feel that they are bound together by an obscure current passing through them. 'For this is not one life; nor do I always know if I am man or woman, Bernard or Neville, Louis, Susan, Jinny, or Rhoda – so strange is the contact of one with another.'[1]

One of the images around which the book started to germinate was Vanessa's description of a huge moth that had come tapping on the window of her house in Cassis, where she sat writing to her sister with 'moths flying madly in circles round me & the lamp'.[2] Woolf took *The Moths* as the working title for her new novel, and she imagined her characters drawn together like moths around a light, an idea that had been with her since the evenings of bug hunting in the garden as a child. In place of the central light Woolf invented a seventh character, Percival. He is absent from the start, someone we know about only through other people. Like Jacob, and like Woolf's brother

Thoby Stephen, this magnetic but elusive young man dies early, leaving his friends to gather round in his memory.

Woolf went back through Thoby's letters as she wrote, and recorded in September 1930 that it would have been his fiftieth birthday. She wondered whether she could write his name and dates at the front of her novel and thus make it explicitly an elegy. But she had wondered the same about *Jacob's Room* and decided against this kind of specific personal tribute. She had not dedicated *To the Lighthouse* to her parents – or to anyone else. 'This shall be Childhood', she said, writing the early section of *The Waves*, 'but it must not be *my* childhood'.[3] So she left her book without a dedication, standing as a universal elegy, and as a novel about the connection between people who have kept one another in mind over many years.

None of the characters is a portrait from life and the book is insistently impersonal, though there are many glimpses here of the people who had meant most to Virginia Woolf. There is Susan with her rural home and her children, envied by the childless Neville; in Louis there is a flickering sight of T. S. Eliot hanging up his cane after work and writing poetry (though the more powerful tribute to Eliot is the web of allusion to *The Waste Land* that runs all through the book). Each of these people is full of idiosyncrasies but impresses the reader at the same time as some kind of archetype. They have lives of their own, but they are representatives too of certain kinds of experience and aspects of personality. So we understand Jinny as a complete individual but also, more generally, as that social self which comes alive at a party, among the lights and the music.

'The six characters were supposed to be one', Woolf wrote.[4] They are the community of her friends, but they are also the whole community of different people whom she felt herself to be. Each of the characters says things that Woolf had said to herself in her diary, and each, for a moment here or there, sounds like her. In the garden at Monk's House she could be Susan; and though Neville the academic classicist lives the kind of establishment life Woolf did not want for herself, he makes the same nervous assessments of his worth, feeling in his pocket for the sheet on which his 'credentials' are written.[5] So *The Waves* develops Clarissa Dalloway's potent idea that we are all many things: 'she would not say of any one in the world now that they were this or were that'.[6] Much of Woolf's writing life was devoted to the undoing of such labels, exposing the falsity involved in defining anyone as 'this' or 'that'.

If the characters of *The Waves* are at some level 'all one', it doesn't matter that we sometimes lose track of who is speaking. It is part of the point of the novel that the voices elide; though they are speaking about different things, they share the same rhythm. 'I am writing to a rhythm and not to a plot', Woolf said.[7] Her evening habit of listening to the gramophone with Leonard became one of the most fertile times of her writing day. Several of her key breakthroughs with difficult passages in the book came while listening to music. Because it is written to a rhythm, Woolf's readers have to beat time. It is no good trying to go too fast: Woolf slows us down to the pace of her characters' acute observations of their world. They watch and perceive with a kind of childish wonder, long after they have grown up. Their monologues are in the present tense, as if they have stopped in the midst of things (as adults so rarely do) for a moment's amazed reflection. *The Waves* may be Woolf's most difficult book, but it is also the one in which we hear most clearly the childlike tone in her voice.

Woolf's friends often remarked on her unjaded curiosity and appetite for detail. It was part of what made her enchanting to children. Vita Sackville-West's son Nigel Nicolson, for example, remembered her asking what had happened to him one day:

'A grain fell and spiralled down; a petal fell, filled and sank. At that the fleet of boat-shaped bodies paused; poised; equipped; mailed; then with a waver of undulation off they flashed.' Fish go darting through Virginia Woolf's writing, as here in *Between the Acts*. The photograph shows Leonard Woolf feeding the fish at Rodmell *c.* 1932 (note the big toffee container being reused here: the Woolfs were very partial to sweets).

> I replied 'Well nothing happened. I have just come
> home from school and here I am.' She said, 'Oh! that
> won't do, start at the beginning. What woke you up?'
> I said 'It was the sun – the sun coming through the
> window of my room at Eton.' Then she said, leaning
> forward very intently, 'What sort of sun was it? Was it a
> cheerful sun or was it an angry sun?' In this sort of way
> we continued to retrace my day minute by minute.[8]

That rising sun with its changing light becomes in Woolf's
hands the lyrical framework for a novel in which there is no
such thing as 'nothing happened'.

The Waves did not come all in a flash as To the Lighthouse
had done. It was trial and error throughout the autumn of 1929,
until Woolf's notebook looked 'like a lunatic's dream'.[9] She
couldn't decide where she stood in relation to her characters:
'am I outside the thinker?'[10] In the New Year she hit her stride,
feeling as if she'd come 'breaking through gorse' to reach the
centre.[11] The image recalled vigorous Stephen family walks
through the dry, gorsy landscape of Cornwall, to which she
was returning in imagination as she wrote the childhood sections of her book. Woolf's images of her own progress were
often this physical. Though she was writing what she called an
'abstract, eyeless book', she went at the task like an athlete or a
racehorse.[12] Her year was arranged in 'laps': the three months
July to September at Rodmell, the winter in London up to
Christmas, the New Year lap up to the spring holiday, the home
strait in London through May and June before leaving again for
summer in Sussex. Intellectual problems were her 'fences' and
she would not shy at them. She was putting herself through her
paces: warming up and then galloping. She took pleasure in her
own efficiency and tenacity, 'going round in the mill'. She was
the romantic genius who wrote at the end of To the Lighthouse

Vanessa Bell's cover for *The Waves*. On the day she finished the novel, 7 February 1931, Woolf looked back with satisfaction to its strange inception: 'I have netted that fin in the waste of waters which appeared to me over the marshes out of my window at Rodmell.'

'I have had my vision', but she was also the worker spurring herself on, laying bets on herself, noting as she resolved a difficult passage in *The Waves* 'I have taken my fence.'[13] It was her choice to do this: she could very well have written an easier book and pleased her readers by repeating a method they had seen before. But she left that to Vita, whose novel *The Edwardians* was making a small fortune for the Press, and took her self-built fences on her own.

Always raising the bar, Woolf measured herself against the great writers of the past. She copied out quotations from Byron; she wrote into *The Waves* an allusive dialogue with Shelley; for a while she read Dante's *Inferno* for half an hour at the end of her morning's writing, weighing its epic scope and rhythm against hers. She kept dipping back into Shakespeare to challenge herself (and to check that he was still better than her; he always was). Thinking of Greek drama, she wanted her own characters to be like 'statues against the sky'.[14] She was still as passionately ambitious for her writing as she had been at twenty-five when she planned to write 'such English as shall one day burn the pages'.[15] And she had the palpable feeling as she wrote *The Waves* that her day had come. Working at Bernard's closing soliloquy, she wanted nothing less than to 'make prose move – yes I swear – as prose has never moved before: from the chuckle and the babble to the rhapsody'.[16]

There were several periods of illness during the writing, but Woolf was able to talk herself into acceptance of them. She could just about believe in the potential creativity of these 'curious intervals', and she was able to cite some encouraging precedents: *A Room of One's Own* had mostly been invented in bed.[17] 'To do nothing is often my most profitable way', she wrote in February 1930, and again in September she accorded value to her 'seasons of silence'.[18] Organizing her affairs with

characteristic practicality, she had done a deal with her illness.
She suffered it: it paid her back.

Woolf finished the book in a state of such intense excitement that her pen could hardly keep up with her mind:

> I wrote the words O Death fifteen minutes ago, having
> reeled across the last ten pages with some moments
> of such intensity & intoxication that I seemed only to
> stumble after my own voice, or almost, after some sort
> of speaker (as when I was mad). I was almost afraid,
> remembering the voices that used to fly ahead.[19]

She was comparing her writing to her illness, but illness is not
invoked here as a measure of pain or fear as it might have been
in previous years. 'Almost afraid', she says: but there is something now that holds fear just at bay.

The other big story of Woolf's life during 1930 and 1931
was her friendship with the composer Ethel Smyth. *The Waves*
is elusive, suggestive, impersonal; the seventy-year-old woman
who came marching in with the New Year of 1930 was loud,
insistent, and usually talking about herself. They had known
about each other for years and had read each other's books
(Smyth produced autobiographies at a great rate), but only
now, inspired by *A Room of One's Own*, had Ethel made contact.
She came to tea at Tavistock Square on 21 February; the foundations of a friendship were laid as she and Virginia were going
up the stairs to the sitting room, they talked 'ceaselessly' for a
further few hours and parted as the major new players in each
other's lives.[20] 'I want to talk and talk and talk', Woolf wrote to
Smyth soon afterwards: 'About music; about love.'[21] And she
did. Many of the most-quoted statements about her life come
from long letters to Ethel in which she would spell out in num-

bered points (echoing Ethel's no-nonsense tone) her attitudes to sex, work, and her past. This was linked with her sense of getting older and starting to assess what she had made of things. But why was it Ethel Smyth with whom she wanted to talk?

Ethel lent herself to caricature. Inevitably Woolf and her surprised friends had a field day with 'the rant and the riot and the egotism' of this large, deaf, outspoken septuagenarian warhorse of the feminist cause.[22] She had once been in prison with Emmeline Pankhurst and had written the suffragist anthem 'The March of the Women'. She had fought for her rights with military pride (she was the daughter of a major-general, as Woolf constantly reminded her). In her lifelong campaign for freedom she had taken just the opposite approach to Woolf's subtle, ironic experimentalism, and Woolf liked her for it. It was one of the defining things about Woolf's life that she loved people (Vita and Ethel especially) who were not at all like herself. She did not need them to understand what she was doing in her writing; and though she wanted their devotion she was always imagining what their lives were like without her. 'Please if I ever come again, dont meet me', she wrote quietly and movingly to Ethel after a visit to her home in Woking, 'let me find you among your things'.[23]

At the height of their relationship, Ethel's letters were daily and extremely long, telegrams frequently arrived in between, and her visits in person – invited or not – came at gale force. The whole effect could feel like 'a circulating thunderstorm'.[24] It was a tremendous distraction from work; only Leonard, Vanessa, and Vita had previously been allowed to take up this much time. 'Should I curtail her?' Woolf wondered, but part of the attraction was Ethel's refusal to compromise.[25] A moderate friendship would be a contradiction in terms. So Woolf let the whole symphony continue, making space for Ethel in her life, and coming to depend on her as one depends on a lover.

Virginia Woolf and Ethel Smyth at Monk's House. Smyth was in her seventies and hard of hearing, but nothing could hinder the stream of talk.

Virginia Woolf was not in love with Ethel Smyth, though Ethel was quite openly in love with her. Virginia was swept up, mothered, challenged, and given new energy, but Ethel did not inspire the kind of fantasies that bubbled up the moment Virginia thought of Vita. For a while she played Vita off against 'that old sea-monster encrusted with barnacles', enjoying the frisson of Vita's jealousy.[26] She wondered about the difference between love and friendship. Society's compulsion to label sexual feelings was one of the things she wrote to Ethel about: 'Where people mistake, as I think, is in perpetually narrowing and naming these immensely composite and wideflung passions – driving stakes through them, herding them between screens.'[27] This discussion with Ethel was a version of the thinking she was doing in *The Waves* about 'composite' and fluid personalities. There can be no screens set up between her silent work in writing that book and the 'talk talk talk' that went on around it.

Though she complained of the constant interruption of 'seeing people', and though her socially packed letters give few clues that she was doing any work at all, Woolf was in fact getting a great deal done. In need of a fantastic excursion in the vein of *Orlando*, she wrote her biography of Flush the spaniel, taking her own spaniel Pinker as a model. It was another tribute to her affair with Vita, especially since Pinker was the offspring of Vita's dog Pippin and since much of their courtship had deferred to canine goings-on as code for their own seductions. Again, half laughing, half serious, she was pushing at the limits of life-writing, arguing for a telling change of perspective, looking up at Elizabeth Barrett Browning from a point of view close to the floor.

Then, straight after *The Waves*, she compiled a second volume of *The Common Reader*, 'furbishing up' twenty-six of her recent essays. Sorting through the critical work she had published since the first *Common Reader* in 1926, she found she had more than a hundred pieces to choose from. She often felt frustrated by her non-fiction, feeling that she had not sufficiently freed herself from the conventions of reviewing, wondering what form might be supple enough to express the experiences of reading. Nonetheless, she is one of the great critics in English.

She liked her essays to sound like a conversation with the reader, and in some cases actually staged a dialogue, as she did with 'Walter Sickert: A Conversation' in 1933. She was not going to tell people what to think of a book, and this form freed her from the self-assertion she loathed. She wanted instead to evoke mood, and to measure what remains in memory when the novel is put away. Take her long essay on Thomas Hardy (first published on his death in 1928 and revised for the second *Common Reader*). She hears 'the sound of a waterfall' booming through an early novel, she sees 'moments of vision' ebbing away into 'stretches of plain daylight'.[28] In every one of Hardy's books, she says, 'three or four figures predominate and stand up like lightning conductors to attract the elements'.[29] Her inexhaustible similes translate abstract impressions into pictures of arresting clarity.

Woolf's essays open up conversations, but one of the people whose conversation about books she most valued was not there to respond. Lytton Strachey was dying at Ham Spray House. She had dedicated the first *Common Reader* to Strachey, and she mourned him as she worked on the second. His absence affected her feelings about Ethel's non-stop presence. At times she just wanted Ethel to shut up. She wanted to associate herself with reflective quietness rather than the shimmering talk for which Bloomsbury had become known. 'Everyone I most honour is silent', she wrote to Ethel pointedly at Christmas 1931.[30]

For years her happiest moments had been quiet ones: 'I like driving off to Rodmell on a hot Friday evening and having cold ham, and sitting on my terrace and smoking a cigar with an owl or two.'[31] In the hot summer of 1930 she had sunk deep into her country life, 'languid as an alligator with only its nostrils above water'.[32] Now she was thickening her carapace again and sliding under. To protect her quietness and autonomy, she turned down numerous invitations to write and speak. She was famous, but she did not want to be in the public eye. There were several books being written about her, but she was either unhelpful or actively hostile to their authors, insisting that her novels must speak for themselves. She was being made into a mosaic for the floor of the National Gallery as part of a modern pantheon (which is still there) and, though she didn't protest, most people would have been more pleased. She wanted to be read, she wanted some money, and she wanted to be free to write what she chose. That was what mattered, and she rejected the other trappings that fame offered her.

Woolf was suspicious of all pomp and ceremony. Where once she had recoiled from George Duckworth's black-tie parties, now she declined official honours, which she saw as part of the same establishment parade. She turned down an honorary doctorate from the University of Manchester. She wrote a long letter to the *New Statesman* explaining her wish to be private, and proposing a 'Society for the Protection of Privacy'.[33] It was a fierce statement, but it was full of conflicting ideas. Even in asserting her privacy she was speaking out, promoting a cause, forming (albeit in parody) a new society. That negotiation between public and private was at the heart of the new novel she was writing at great length and compulsive speed. When in 1932 the University of Cambridge asked her to give the prestigious Clark Lectures, which her father had given in 1888, she paused to think. But no, she decided, she would not give the Clark Lectures at Trinity (where once she had been shooed off the grass). What she wanted to talk about now was not the kind of thing the dons of Trinity would want to hear.

9   The Argument of Art   1932–1938

Woolf wrote the first draft of *The Pargiters* in great excitement. This was the novel that would become *The Years* and she had a version of it finished by September 1934. It was enormous: 900 pages, about 200,000 words, and she knew it would have to be 'sweated down'. But she was pleased with it.

The book was extremely ambitious: 'I want to give the whole of present society', Woolf wrote, 'nothing less: facts, as well as the vision. And to combine them both. I mean, The Waves going on simultaneously with Night & Day.'[1] So this was a bringing together of all she had done so far, calling on the visionary qualities she had developed in *The Waves* to give meaning to the kind of realism she had used in her early novels. She was thinking back over her writing life, and back over her family life as well. This novel took her again to the dark rooms of Kensington, which become here the home of the Pargiter family at Abercorn Terrace. A mother lies dying slowly in the sick room upstairs; restless daughters wait for the kettle to boil. Then the novel skips forward into the twentieth century and finds the daughters moving off across London, selling the old house, making lives for themselves, facing choices about their homes, work, friends, politics. She would bring it right up to the present, gathering together 'millions of ideas': 'a summing up of all I know, feel, laugh at, despise, like, admire, hate'.[2]

Woolf was taking on the tradition of historical fiction and turning it around. Her contemporaries John Galsworthy and Hugh Walpole were writing lengthy family sagas (*The Forsyte Saga*; the Herries novels) which sold in great numbers. Woolf too might have written this kind of history, and Hyde Park Gate alone suggested material enough for many volumes. But she chose instead to open up the genre for examination, and wrote a series of extracts which pretended to be from a continuous family history. Instead of pressing on through year after year, she isolated moments – from 1880, 1891, 1907, and so on – taking their temperature, giving a cross-section of life, catching the atmosphere very concisely 'plumb in the centre'.[3]

At first she set up around these episodes a framework narrative which involved a novelist reading out extracts from her book and then using them to illustrate a lecture about women's lives. In parody of the prolix saga writer, this novelist begins solemnly with an extract from volume five. It was a nice joke, but serious too. Woolf's lecture-with-extracts format allowed for the meeting of fact and fiction, analysis and creativity, the voice of the critic and the novelist – all in the same book. It was a potent idea, but she changed her mind. She worried about the fiction being mixed up with a lecture; she didn't want to be a writer of propaganda. And yet there were things she wanted to say. The question, as she posed it to herself, was how to give 'intellectual argument in the form of art'.[4]

In the end Woolf separated out the 'novel' from the 'essay'. The argument of the lecture did not disappear (it would come back, more intense and disturbing, in *Three Guineas*), but for now she was left with her scenes from a family history. The problem was that they threatened to get longer than the sagas she parodied. She turned for help to the masters of long novels, the Russians. She weighed Dostoevsky's inclusiveness against

Turgenev's paring down. As she read Turgenev she could see him coming up against her own problems and finding ways, like her, to combine the factual elements of daily life with 'the vision'.[5] Turning back to her own draft, she cut and cut but still the novel grew. She packed it with details of the kind that had been filling her diary for years, from the headlines on newspaper placards and the character of the Bayswater Road, to the sound of pigeons ('take two coos, Taffy; take two') and the little customary lies that people tell every day. She caught the tone and texture of objects, buildings, chairs, coats, shoes, the scenery and props of each successive age. *The Years* is not often compared to the fun and games of *Orlando* but Woolf associated the two novels from the start. 'In truth The Pargiters is first cousin to Orlando,' she mused in her diary: 'Orlando taught me the trick of it.'[6] She had all the same sense of momentum and drama, wanting to make 'agile leaps, like a chamois across precipices from 1880 to here & now'. As she raced through the first draft she was 'incandescent' with the thrill of it.[7]

Long accused of social narrowness, here she described lodging houses and charity work, the dirty man from Wandsworth, and (notoriously) the greasy Jew.[8] With bracing, sometimes repellent honesty, bound to incite rather than allay her critics, she recorded prejudice and snobbery as part of the fabric of life. And for the first time she gave sustained voice to a servant, faithful Crosby. Woolf's own relationship with servants had itself been a long-drawn-out saga, which reached a painful climax when she finally sacked her live-in servant Nelly in 1934 and started a new rhythm of life with daily helps.[9] Her mixed feelings for Nelly shaped her portrait of Crosby. When Eleanor in *The Years* lets Crosby go and clears her room, she realizes with guilty horror the dinginess of the servants' quarters in the basement. This was difficult material and Woolf wanted to tackle it.

She had never been 'more excited over a book', but just as she neared the end of the draft, there was a blow.[10] Roger Fry fell over on 7 September 1934 and died two days later. Woolf sensed all the 'substance' going out of her world.[11] Fry's aesthetics had been a deep, sustained influence on her writing, and his friendship had been a tonic to her. He always exuded energy and talked passionately about the arts. In the sad months after Lytton's death, the Woolfs had found it a great relief to go travelling in Greece with Roger and his sister, spurred on by Fry's gift for making the best of life. With his death, another voice had stopped. 'Oh how we've talked and talked – for 20 years now', Woolf told Ethel sadly.[12]

She was moved by Fry's funeral and the solidarity of those gathered in his memory. It was the feeling of connection she had written about after Percival's death in *The Waves*. Though she rejected the overblown rituals of Victorian mourning that had seemed so dishonest to her as a child, she always felt the need to mark endings and pay tribute. Lytton Strachey had defied convention by asking not to have a funeral, which seemed to Woolf to leave only a dissipated silence. Fry's funeral, all done in music, seemed a better answer to those questions Woolf never stopped asking about how significant moments should be marked in a secular age.

With Fry gone, and the death of another friend, Frances Birrell, in the New Year of 1935, Woolf felt surrounded by ghosts. People were starting to write about the end of Bloomsbury. Part of it *was* gone. In January there was a high-spirited party in the old style, with a performance of *Freshwater*, the comic play about their Victorian ancestors that Woolf had first written in the early 1920s and now revised for the occasion. There was Vanessa as Julia Margaret Cameron and Adrian as Tennyson, striding around reciting things. Everyone laughed, but they were aware of absent friends. By chance someone

'How the ghost of Roger haunted us!' Fry had been one of Woolf's closest friends and his ideas about art had a profound influence on her writing.

came to return one of Fry's paintings in the middle of the rehearsal. Sad and haunted, Woolf noted in her diary: 'Roger's ghost knocked at the door.'[13] Sometimes she felt posthumous herself. Students were writing their theses on her; Stephen Tomlin came to sculpt her face and cast her in bronze. She had to keep telling herself that she was only just starting out. At intervals she vowed in her diary that she would 'go on adventuring, changing, opening my mind & my eyes, refusing to be stamped & stereotyped'.[14]

She wanted nonetheless to honour and defend her past. For years she had been thinking about ways to write portraits of her friends, and now she was called on as Bloomsbury's biographer. The Strachey family had wanted her to write about Lytton, though somehow they hadn't liked to ask her. Fry's family was more forthcoming with the invitation, handing over piles of letters, wanting her opinions, setting out what should and shouldn't be included. So in 1935, as Woolf started to rewrite *The Pargiters*, another book was already coming into view and the biographer's long process of reading, collecting, and interviewing went on in the background as she wrote her fiction. The same questions came up in both. How do public lives relate to the private? How much can be said? Could she, for instance, write about the love affair Fry had once had with Vanessa? Fry's family said 'no', in contrast to Vanessa's insistence on truth. Woolf felt some of the old frustration at the hushing up and covering over. She wrote this repression into her fiction, where people open their mouths to say things and then get stuck halfway.

She dashed through a first 'wild re-typing' of her novel and then slowed down for a second revision.[15] She paced herself and enjoyed it, typing up her changes every morning and packing her afternoons full with other people and other projects. As a counter to their awareness of getting older and the loss of friends, she and Leonard were very active. They did ambitious trips in their new car; there were new friends like Elizabeth Bowen, and Virginia warmed to the strange, striking Sitwells. She was more intimate now with T. S. Eliot. She never felt much at ease with her brother Adrian, but she enjoyed being an aunt to his daughters Ann and Judith, now growing up and going off confidently to university. The qualities of Mitzi, Leonard's new pet marmoset, were more dubious, but having arrived in a sickly state from the Rothschild estate, Mitzi quickly learned the ways of Bloomsbury sociability and was always on the scene.

In her diary for 15 October 1935, Woolf listed the things she had done since getting back from Monk's House ten days before. We get a shorthand cross-section of a working week:

> Seen: Janie, Walther; Joan Easedale; Nessa. Clive.
> Helen. Duncan. been to Richmond Park (saw snake
> by the Serpentine) Concert. Saw Morgan & Bob &
> Eth Williamson. Asked to speak at some lunch. Read
> all early R. letters. noted them. also library books:
> also Keats: also MSS.

It doesn't take much filling out of the abbreviations to sense the variety and busyness here. Janie Bussy and François Walter had come to discuss an anti-Fascist organization; she was assembling her material for the Fry biography; she was reading, as ever, through the manuscripts of possible books for the Hogarth Press. This is all in addition to 'forging ahead' with *The Years*, and it counts as a time of 'calm full complete bliss'.[16] Woolf was happy because the novel was going well. She wrote the last line of the second draft in December. 'The main feeling about this book is vitality, fruitfulness, energy,' she concluded in her diary. 'Never did I enjoy writing a book more.'[17]

Edith Sitwell recording a poetry reading in March 1927. Woolf and Sitwell were never close but they admired each other at a distance.

The disaster began soon after she wrote that last line. A headache started, and her images for the novel turned from vitality to disease. To be rid of it would be like having a 'bag of muscle [...] cut out of my brain'.[18] She hated reading back through it, and laboured over her corrections in despair. Leonard made her stop in May for a holiday and took her to Cornwall, as he had done at previous times of crisis. But the ritual pilgrimage did not save her from collapse. It was the worst since the breakdown of 1913. She lost weight fast and couldn't sleep. Back at Monk's House for the summer, she tried to do half an hour at a time on her proofs – 600 pages sitting in an accusatory unread pile – but she struggled to achieve even that. It seems probable that the menopause exacerbated this breakdown; certainly it brought physical symptoms that weakened her. She had long wondered whether this would be a dangerous time, and it was. But for her the end of a novel was always a dangerous time as well, and both took their toll on her health. She was back to short walks, rest, and disciplined eating.

In the autumn she could gingerly attempt the proofs again and she kept at it. She went grimly to the end before taking the whole pile to Leonard. She felt like a cat bringing in a dead mouse. She asked him to burn it and arranged to cover the wasted printing costs from her savings. Leonard asked her to wait until he had read it. The pressure on him was enormous: everything depended on what he thought. She watched for signals as he read. At last, on 5 November, he put the book down in tears and pronounced it remarkable. To Virginia this seemed like a miracle: 'the moment of relief was divine'.[19] With catastrophe averted, they went out together to Lewes to see the great Bonfire Night parade. *The Years* was to be published after all. Woolf prepared herself not to mind the reviews. Whatever they said, she had finished the book and survived.

She paused to acknowledge the achievement in her diary: 'I hand my compliment to that terribly depressed woman, myself, whose head ached so often: who was so entirely convinced a failure; for in spite of everything I think she brought it off.'[20]

Because this book brought Woolf close to suicide, because it was connected with the politics of the mid-1930s and with its ferocious non-fiction counterpart *Three Guineas*, and because its formal patternings have more to do with breakage and disconnection than with visionary wholeness, *The Years* is usually talked about in sober terms. Critics emphasize the failure and suffering of the characters, as well as the failure and suffering of their author. They note a complete contrast to *The Waves*: a move from the inner world to the outer, and from lyricism to a complex realism. It is the least read and least taught of Woolf's novels; its general readers are few and far between.

And yet in Woolf's lifetime it was the fastest-selling of her books and the only one to reach the bestseller lists in America. She explicitly said that she wanted to attract the general reader, almost in recompense for the obscurity of *The Waves* – and because she did after all think 'the common reader' was important. We should remember as well the 'vitality' and 'fruitfulness' she thought characterized the novel.[21] Her turn to 'facts' was prompted by her 'infinite delight' in them, and her pleasure in recording some of that great storehouse of daily observations she had been making for forty years.

She allowed her facts, in places, to be extremely beautiful, revealing her aesthetic pleasure in ordinary things. The book has a glimmering quality about it, a sense of significance we can't quite grasp. Its characters try to articulate their visions of 'a different life', 'another world'.[22] The search for some underlying pattern continues here: 'Who makes it?' asks Eleanor. 'Who thinks it?'[23] Woolf wanted both the past and the future to be palpable, and she even thought of calling the novel *Dawn*. She censored this romantic impulse, but the new day dawning over London at the close brings an obscure, uplifting hope as Eleanor watches a young couple on the threshold of their home and their lives. Where the last line of *The Waves* is a call to battle against death, *The Years* ends with the sky brightening over the city, bringing 'beauty, simplicity and peace'.[24]

But this is also a dark book that readers have long found troubling. Its moments of beauty are mixed up with disfigurement, prejudice, powerlessness, claustrophobia. Lyricism is often purposely curtailed, leaving awkward gaps and repetitions. Almost every page is marked by some failure of communication. People mishear and misunderstand each other; ideas are passed on like Chinese whispers, getting distorted along the way. At the final party Eleanor looks around at people talking and wonders how often we really listen to each other.

The novel is in part about this distraction and inattentiveness, which Woolf noticed all around her in the 1930s. Europe was heading towards crisis and everyone was talking about it, but what was actually to be done? Politics distracted her from writing; her writing distracted her from politics. She took several newspapers and read them compulsively; she thought carefully about her pacifism, she talked daily with Leonard, whose life was now devoted to politics. Yet in a moment of characteristic self-scrutiny she noted that while talking with Maynard Keynes in 1934 about the situation in Germany, she was actually thinking all the time about her novel. As the situation escalated in the mid-1930s she became increasingly involved with campaign groups and worried over whether she might be doing more. But fundamentally her novel *was* her political work. As she would say during the war, 'thinking is my fighting'.[25]

Woolf's nephew Julian Bell with his friend John Lehmann, who worked for
the Hogarth Press and bought Virginia's share of it in 1938.

She was surrounded by people who were challenging her position. Leonard found pacifism increasingly unrealistic. The young men she knew through her nephew Julian and the Hogarth Press manager John Lehmann were all committed to an active fight against Fascism. They were also mobilizing literature for the cause: Auden, Spender, Isherwood all saw their art working in the service of politics. They respected Virginia Woolf, their great literary forebear, but they disagreed with her. She responded with a complicated mixture of generosity, anxiety, and detachment. They seemed to her egotistical, overrating their importance. Stephen Spender, for example, told her that the Communist Party officials rather hoped he would die tragically and be their Byron. Woolf suspected that too much of this hero hunting was going on.

The most testing relationship was with Julian himself. She wanted a close friendship with him, but she refused to be his literary mentor and found it impossible to praise his poetry. True she didn't like it, but she might have lied. Instead she rejected in an offhand way a long essay on Roger Fry over which Julian had taken great care. This in turn strained her relationship with Vanessa. No one wanted this awkwardness, so why keep causing it?

Part of it was defensiveness. Julian's insistence on action made Woolf uneasy. She caricatured herself as the unworldly poet, but would then suddenly assert her political engagement. In June 1936 she sent Julian a jokey but acid description of the mood at Charleston, pretending to side with him against Vanessa and Duncan's passivity: 'There they sit, looking at pinks and yellows, and when Europe blazes all they do is screw up their eyes and complain of a temporary glare in the foreground.'[26] Was this hypocrisy? Wasn't *she* sitting too? Yes, but she was writing. Was that enough? When she used the image three years later in *Between the Acts* the dynamics had shifted.

Julian Bell and Roger Fry playing chess at Charleston, painted by Vanessa
Bell. There were loving discussions between the generations of Bloomsbury,
but there were also disagreements. Julian argued against the pacifism of his
parents and many of their friends, calling for military action against Fascism
in the 1930s.

Giles rages at the passivity of his family as they sit around looking at the view, but it is quite clear that he is impotent as well. His anger does not achieve anything and the villagers who peacefully act out their play in the old tradition while it's still possible seem perhaps to be doing something more worthwhile than him.

So even in her last novel Woolf was still opposing herself to Julian, but by this time he was dead. He joined the International Brigade against Franco in 1937 and was killed that July. Vanessa was distraught. Her children were unconditionally the centre of her life, and this was a loss from which she would never recover. Virginia stepped in as a devoted support for her sister, and she kept trying to understand why Julian had gone to Spain at all. Without him, the future seemed 'lopped: deformed'.[27]

In the midst of this sadness Woolf was thankful for her own life with Leonard. Several times Leonard had to see specialists about his health, leaving her to pace up and down outside the consulting rooms imagining the worst. When he was given the all-clear, she was overwhelmed with relief, as she had been after the crisis of *The Years*. They had both had their trials and been granted reprieves. They walked around Tavistock Square 'love-making' as they had done twenty-five years before.[28] She felt a rush of vitality, as if making up for the time she had lost to illness and to the long grind of her novel.

She used this energy to write the book-length essay *Three Guineas*, in which she considered the economic and political roles of women and proposed profound structural shifts in social organization that might be more effective than bombs in the fight against Fascism. It was radical but subtle, it was fierce yet indirect. It was long and involved precisely because Woolf mistrusted the bald statements of propaganda. She saw the problems of the present as intractably linked with the behaviour of the middle classes, of both genders, in private and in public, over the past hundred years. *Three Guineas* suggested that Hitler was only the most violent manifestation of a form of tyranny in which *all* patriarchal society was complicit.

Many of Woolf's friends thought *Three Guineas* an embarrassment and an aberration. Yet it was not a sudden outburst. Woolf saw it as a continuation of *A Room of One's Own*, so it reached back to the 1920s and far beyond that to the repressions of Hyde Park Gate. It was shaped by her continuing conversations with Ethel Smyth, and it was something she had been preparing for all through the 1930s as she amassed cuttings from newspapers, manifestos, memoirs – a massive store of exhibits that she held up for examination as she put contemporary society on trial. The pressure of argument had been building in her for years and now it poured out 'like a physical volcano'.[29]

Woolf's conceptual sweep took in family relations, education, law, church, and government. As in *The Years* she showed that domestic spaces are powerfully political, and she followed their dynamics out of the front door into public life. She printed in her book a series of photographs of men in their uniforms: a wigged lawyer, dons processing, a bishop in his mitre. Encountered in the law court or university, these are figures of unchallenged power, but encountered in Woolf's book they look plain ridiculous. Woolf was holding the judges up to judgment and liberating the 'outsider' (who has no uniform) from the inhibiting attitude of hushed reverence.

Like the characters in her fiction, Woolf was feeling towards a different way of doing things. It would require new social relations and new voices. It could not be definitively articulated, but a beginning could be made. Having stated her case, Woolf closed the book with relief. When people asked for her opinions now, she could refer them to *Three Guineas*. She felt released from a burden and free to think of something else. It was the feeling she gave to Peggy Pargiter near the end of *The Years*:

CHAPTER 9

She had not said it, but she had tried to say it. Now
she could rest; now she could think herself away under
the shadow of their ridicule, which had no power to
hurt her, into the country. Her eyes half shut; it seemed
to her that she was on a terrace, in the evening; an
owl went up and down, up and down; its white wing
showed on the dark of the hedge; and she heard
country people singing and the rattle of wheels on
a road.[30]

10 Sussex 1938–1941

In the summer of 1938 the Woolfs had a new room built into the roof at Monk's House, with a veranda so they could read outside in the evenings. It was hot and peaceful, and Virginia started contentedly on the fourteen volumes of Madame de Sévigné's letters. She took her long walks over the Downs each afternoon, then there was dinner and bowls on the lawn, followed by music on the gramophone and more reading. She thought about how to live freely and expansively as she got older. She was fifty-six, and made plans for the next ten years.

But when she turned on the radio everything was different. There was the 'violent rant' and 'savage howl' of Adolf Hitler.[1] She thought back to August 1914, except that this time there was no illusion about an honourable war over by Christmas. This time it felt as if they were all 'slipping consciously into a pit'.[2] As ever she had the old tensions of Hyde Park Gate in mind as the measure for her emotions. She was a powerless child again, waiting for the worst to happen: 'As for politics, I feel as if we were all sitting downstairs while someone slowly dies.'[3] That autumn came the guilty reprieve of the Munich crisis. The weather held until October, but each fine day felt as if it must be the last.

Woolf was immersed in writing *Roger Fry* and thankful for it. She was glad to think about Fry rather than Hitler every morning, and admired him more and more as she went on. But it was hard work. She did huge amounts of research and rewriting, and wrestled with the problem of how to keep a vivid impression of the living man in the foreground while also setting down all the necessary facts. 'How to keep the flight of the mind, yet be exact?' she asked herself.[4] It was typical of her conscientiousness that even after all this reading she felt unqualified to comment on Fry's painting. Hence her request to Duncan Grant that he provide a 'technical appreciation' of Fry's painting to be printed as an appendix (which in the end was not very technical and did not say anything she could not have said herself). Her anxiety was linked with her sense of responsibility to those who had loved Fry, and her realization that she was shaping his posthumous reputation. As she noted when the book was published, it was as if she and he together 'had given birth to this vision of him' and yet he had no power to alter it.[5]

In representing him she suppressed herself, even to the extent of referring to Virginia Woolf in the third person. The concern with impersonality that had long shaped her approach to fiction, and which she articulated in her letters to Ethel, was again important in the biography. Woolf was known for her experiments in life-writing: here was the woman who had written lives of Orlando and of Flush, and whose numerous reviews of other people's biographies had proposed new ways of conveying character. Yet now with a biography of Roger to write, she wanted *his* experiments to be the focus of attention, not hers. Her own role she saw as that of the craftsman, like a carpenter perhaps. She was making something and she would make it well, even when that meant months of 'grind' and 'drudgery' and seemed 'appallingly difficult'.[6]

Roger Fry has often been thought too traditional to be of much literary interest, and certainly it does not wear innovation

'The view across the meadows to Caburn is before me now.' Woolf is one of the great writers of place. Whenever she was at Monk's House, she walked daily across the surrounding marshes, farmland, and downs.

on its sleeve. But Woolf puts to good use here some of the great discoveries of her writing life. She is the author of *Jacob's Room* itemizing the clutter in Fry's studio and leaving us to divine the kind of life that is led there. She is the author of *To the Lighthouse*, relegating the bald statement of Helen Fry's death to a footnote, or repeatedly invoking the 'hidden centre' of Fry's life and the 'moments of vision' in which he sees his way through.[7] Though she presses back her own feeling, there are passages where Woolf's sympathy is near the surface. When Fry's wife is taken to an asylum, for example: 'he found, as he was often to find in the future, that the only way of facing the ruin of private happiness was to work'.[8] And she copied out a comment he made as life closed in during the 1914–18 war: 'Oh the boredom of war – the ways of killing men are so monotonous compared to the ways of living.'[9]

She finished her first draft in March 1939 and revised it through another hot summer of daily incongruities, her immediate life seeming so much more real and absorbing than the mad, monotonous, shouting voice of Hitler on the radio. She was on edge – like most people that summer. There was the added tension of moving house, because building work around Tavistock Square made it so noisy. Everything was packed up and transplanted to a flat in nearby Mecklenburgh Square, but London was so full of anxieties that the Woolfs left most of their possessions in boxes and went to Monk's House. Their tiredness showed itself in fractious exchanges. Leonard wanted a greenhouse and Virginia didn't, which turned into an argument that neither of them wanted to have.

The Sussex landscape, by contrast, seemed to Virginia more peaceful and beautiful than ever. In August, on what she thought would be the last day of peace, she lay under a cornstack watching 'the empty land & the pinkish clouds'.[10] For the first time since her illness in 1913 she and Leonard stayed in

Sussex for the autumn and winter rather than go back to London. Settling into a rhythm of country life, they became more involved with the village. Neighbours popped in to chat at all the wrong times, Virginia was elected treasurer of the Women's Institute and was roped into helping with the village play, there was First Aid practice at the rectory, Leonard joined the home guard and gave away their saucepans to be made into aeroplanes, a policeman came to tell them off for careless-ness with their blackout curtains, the grocer gave them an extra ration of tea. Rodmell rivalled Bloomsbury in the art of gossip. There was said to be a nun on the bus who paid her fare with a man's hand.

The village people grew to like Mrs Woolf, though she could look very odd talking to herself on her long walks and she could be short-tempered or distracted. She in turn had very mixed feelings about the village. At times she expressed with disturbing ferocity her sense of being sucked dry by people who could give her nothing back. Yet, coming across the marsh from the Downs in the evening, she loved to see the lights close together, offering shelter. This fundamental idea of community appealed to her very deeply, and she wanted to write about it.

All the time she was working on the biography she was also thinking about a novel. As she had often found before, she needed several books on the go so that one might provide a rest and a change from the other ('rotating my crops', as she once told herself).[11] Her new novel, *Pointz Hall* (she changed the title at the last moment to *Between the Acts*), was about a village pageant staged in the grounds of an old house in June 1939. It was set over the course of a single day, which connected it back to *Mrs Dalloway*, though here the intensely evoked setting was not London but rural downland. In the still air a cow is heard coughing in the distance; in the mid-afternoon a butterfly suns itself sensuously 'on a sunlit yellow plate'.[12] The mood is festive.

Paper garlands are strung across the barn; tea is laid out for the audience and actors.

Woolf, looking out at the countryside in Sussex, was aware of what she called 'a kind of growl behind the cuckoo and t'other birds: a furnace behind the sky'.[13] She attended to the daily concerns of money, cooking, writing, but there was always this sense of the furnace just out of sight. And it burns behind the peaceful, civilized foreground of *Between the Acts*. In the fragments of talk we overhear as the local people gather for the play, worries about a new cesspool are mixed up with the prospect of invasion. Passion and violence flash out through any chink left open, but no one tone is allowed to dominate for long. It is comic when a sudden shower gives the audience a mid-performance soaking, but it is also, just for a moment, a vision of infinite grief: 'Down it poured like all the people in the world weeping. Tears, Tears. Tears.'[14]

Between the Acts is made of interruptions like this one: conversations cut off, lines forgotten. People keep talking and shuffling during the play. Scenes keep being disrupted and then reconvened. The effect is like a kaleidoscope with beads falling into new patterns. The novel has in places the intensity of a life (the life of rural England) passing in front of one's eyes before it ends. In other places it has the stumbling digressiveness of someone dying slowly, talking quietly about the weather, with each word weighted by the sense of an ending. One of the most ominous interruptions comes when the vicar is making a speech at the end of the pageant. He pauses, he listens: 'did he hear some distant music?' He continues, but then the word 'opportunity' is cut in two as he says it, because it was not music he heard but 'twelve aeroplanes in perfect formation'.[15] 'Then zoom became drone', the planes go by, the speech continues, collection boxes are passed around in the audience, attention is turned to something new.

The Hedge Hoppers, August 18th 1940, by Diana Gardner, a neighbour of
the Woolfs at Rodmell. Woolf recorded the scene in her diary: 'Yesterday,
18th, Sunday, there was a roar. Right on top of us they came. I looked at the
plane, like a minnow at a roaring shark. Over they flashed [...] said to be 5
bombers hedge hopping on their way to London. The closest shave so far.'

In June 1939 those planes were in training, but a year later, as Woolf revised the book at Monk's House, the Battle of Britain was going on in the sky above Sussex. In July: 'I open my window when I hear the Germans, & the broad stalks of light rise all over the meadow feeling for them'.[16] Then in August: 'We lay flat on our faces, hands behind head. Dont close yr teeth said L.' Bombs shook the windows of her writing room. 'A horse neighed on the marsh. Very sultry. Is it thunder? I said. No guns, said L. from Ringmer, from Charleston way.'[17] She phoned Vita, who had bombs falling all around her at Sissinghurst.

In the autumn she went up to look around London. Fifty-two Tavistock Square was destroyed; she could see just a bit of her studio wall still standing, and otherwise 'rubble where I wrote so many books'.[18] There was some strange relief in seeing it in ruins, as if the inevitable had happened and made a clean break of it. The house in Mecklenburgh Square was all 'litter, glass, black soft dust, plaster powder'.[19]

Leonard and Virginia discussed how to die. When the invasion came they would have to act quickly because a Jewish intellectual and his novelist wife could expect the very worst from the Nazis. Soberly, they planned to go to the garage together, shut the doors, and breathe the fumes from the car. Leonard bought extra petrol for the purpose. Later, Adrian was able to get them lethal doses of morphine to use instead. In this context the overhead raids were not especially frightening. As the zooming receded one night Virginia reflected that it would have been 'a peaceful matter of fact death to be popped off on the terrace playing bowls this very fine cool sunny August evening'.[20] 'Matter of fact' became one of her phrases, though the constant tension was affecting her. She found that her hand was shaking. She was reading even more things at once than usual because her mood kept changing. She would dip in and then move on. It was a restlessness she had written about: Isa in *Between the Acts* looks agitatedly around the library, like someone in a chemist's shop needing a remedy for toothache. 'Oughtn't I to read Shakespeare?' Woolf wondered, thinking to end on a high. But she found it hard to concentrate.[21]

She was moving between different pieces of writing as well. She was taking on commissions for essays and short stories, feeling that she should earn money and wanting the sense of a readership at this time when writing could feel useless. At the same time she saw *Roger Fry* through publication, revised *Between the Acts*, and worked on two big new projects. Her response to a time of crisis was the same as Fry's had been: 'must work'.

Just before the war she had started notes for a memoir, having been warned by Vanessa that if she didn't do it now it would get too late. There was certainly no shortage of material. She had the twenty-four volumes of her diary, containing one of the most intricate records of a life ever made. These she left, with hundreds of other manuscripts and papers, in the flat in Mecklenburgh Square in 1939, and there they sat when the Square was bombed, so they were very nearly lost. Woolf salvaged them from the debris before the house was completely destroyed and intended to make use of them eventually. But her memoir began with childhood and depended on other sources: her parents' letters, and her own still-vivid memories. So she went back again to those early years.

This writing of the past made the distracted life of 1939 and 1940 seem more substantial to her. It gave her a sense of depth and trajectory: she was consciously 'getting the past to shadow this broken surface'.[22] She could turn from the debris of her bombed house to write about summers at St Ives, or she could think her way through the rooms of Hyde Park Gate, listing every bit of furniture. She was acutely aware of what she was trying to do for herself by writing this memoir at this time. These apparently casual notes for 'Sketch of the Past' (which she threw into the wastepaper basket by mistake and then retrieved) contain some of her most penetrating comments about her writing life. It is here that she describes her 'shock-receiving capacity', and her intimation of a pattern behind the 'cotton wool'.

She went on writing out the vivid scenes that had remained intact in her mind through the years, and imagining as well the scenes she didn't see: her parents' lives before her birth, and the conversations between adults that had gone on while she was in the nursery. As she had done in *To the Lighthouse*, she was trying to see her parents and siblings on their own terms as well as from the child's point of view. What motivated them? What made that strange 'machine' of the Victorian household go on as it did? She knew that in writing *To the Lighthouse* she had 'rubbed out' some of the force of her parents' memory, but it was far from erased.[23] The memoir kept circling outward and then leading inevitably, irresistibly, back to Julia's death. Then, as Woolf's focus moved on to her father, she found that she was still angry with him, still writing out her physical rage at his behaviour. She used a raw language of 'horror', 'torture', 'brutality'.[24] Vanessa had hated him and rejected him, but Virginia was caught in the more complicated and persistent state of 'ambivalence' (she took the word from Freud, whose work she was now reading for the first time though she had long been aware of his ideas). Her anger was disturbing because she also still loved her father, 'this unworldly, very distinguished and lonely man'.[25]

There was no external need for Virginia Woolf to confront this painful past in November 1940. She made herself do it, shying round it at first, then 'plunging' in. Once she was in it she was caught and held there. Her images are of physical traps.

She imagined George Duckworth and his social demands as a torturous contraption holding her with sharp teeth.[26] The memoir which had started as a holiday from other work seemed to be closing in as well. At the same time, Woolf was reaching the end of *Pointz Hall* and that vulnerable period which accompanied the end of a novel. Seeing the risk and knowing that she needed to think of something different, she immediately turned to the next book, which was already (like Miss La Trobe's next play at the end of *Between the Acts*) rising 'to the surface'.[27]

It was to be a history of literature, starting right at the beginning with a man in the woods listening to birdsong. She was full of plans and excitement about it. Like *Pointz Hall*, to which it was closely connected, it was to be partly a summing up: a celebration of literature 'as I've read it & noted it during the past 20 years'.[28] It was a celebration of her places too. She wanted to show the English landscape changing and shaping the literature that was written and read in it. She wanted to think about writers and their 'backgrounds' – the views from their windows as they work.[29] Even though she had written so much about England in *Pointz Hall*, she kept wanting to describe it rapturously. In her diary she wondered at its 'incredible loveliness': 'How England consoles and warms one.'[30] In the new book she evoked the countryside of the medieval poets, imagining an anonymous figure bringing his lyrics over the Downs, along paths deep in mud, from the cottages to the manor house, where he sang at the back door. She described London at a time when there were fields beyond Bankside. She imagined the actors on their outdoor stage and the crowds cheering in the penny seats. She called this first chapter 'Anon', associating the culture of the Middle Ages with an instinctive community feeling. These were writers who did not even think to give their names.

This selflessness was important to Woolf. Since her earliest diaries she had criticized and controlled her own egotism.[31] Through her years as a famous writer she had refused photographs and interviews. 'Sketch of the Past' is a memoir which strenuously reconstructs *other* people's points of view to test her own. She traced the source of all this to her father. She had learned, she said, at least one lesson from his self-centred behaviour: 'that nothing is so much to be dreaded as egotism'.[32] So, as she continued to do battle with him in 1940, she put the word 'Anon' at the head of her page. In the next chapter she again shifted the emphasis away from the personality of the writer and called it simply 'The Reader'.

She wanted to go on with this book, but if she had to die this seemed a fitting place to stop. 'By the time I've reached Shakespeare the bombs will be falling', she told Ethel, 'So I've arranged a very nice last scene: reading Shakespeare, having forgotten my gas mask, I shall fade far away and quite forget…'[33] Those words from Keats's 'Ode to a Nightingale' had been in her mind as she wrote *Between the Acts* as well. Isa, looking for a quotation, finds that this fantasy of oblivion is the first thing that comes into her head:

Fade far away, dissolve, and quite forget
What thou among the leaves hast never known,
The weariness, the fever, and the fret
Here, where men sit and hear each other groan.

By January 1941, for all her joy in writing, Woolf was struggling against profound despair. She acknowledged it in the diary, swearing that it would not 'engulf' her.[34] She carried on entertaining, writing letters, and correcting the typescript of *Between the Acts*, and there was laughter at Monk's House when Elizabeth Bowen came for the weekend. On 25 February

Woolf finished her corrections and gave the novel to Leonard. Her health went downhill quickly after that. Needing to get through the hours without thinking too much, she set herself physical tasks. It helped to be moving around, so she scrubbed floors and vigorously arranged books. The mass of papers and possessions that had been moved down from London made the house feel oppressively full. She tried to put things in order, but she couldn't find a calm place to settle. She asked for Hogarth Press manuscripts to read as a distraction, but her mind kept racing off.

On 18 March she returned soaking wet from a walk. Leonard found her on her way back through the garden and was alarmed. He tried to get her on to the regime of complete rest to which they had resorted many times before, but it was difficult to impose. The following week he made an urgent appointment with Dr Octavia Wilberforce in Brighton, who found Virginia very thin, very restless, and strangely remote as if she were sleepwalking. Wilberforce was disturbed, but there was not much she could prescribe except rest.

The next morning, Friday 28 March, Virginia sat in her lodge and wrote a letter for Leonard. 'You have given me complete happiness', she told him.

> But I know that I shall never get over this: & I am
> wasting your life […] All I want to say is that until this
> disease came on we were perfectly happy. It was all due
> to you. No one could have been so good as you have
> been. From the very first day till now.[35]

She put this on the sitting-room table, next to a letter for Vanessa that she had written in preparation the previous Sunday. 'I have fought against it,' she wrote to her sister, 'but I can't any longer.'[36] She was resigned to a lonely death, one that

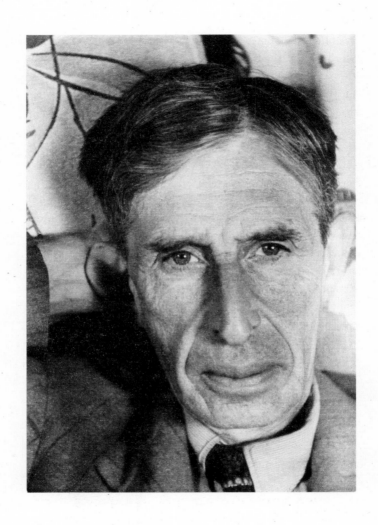

Leonard Woolf by Gisèle Freund.

she could not discuss with either of them. It was not the joint end in the garage she had planned with Leonard; or the 'very nice scene' fading far away with Shakespeare. Because of her illness, and because of the consequent burden of care that she dreaded placing on Leonard again, she decided to die. She put on her wellingtons and fur coat, took her walking stick, and went out across the garden towards the river. She left her stick on the bank and pushed a large stone into her coat pocket. She drowned herself in the very cold, fast-flowing water.

For a long while she disappeared. Her body was not found until more than three weeks later, by which time the winter had become spring. A group of picnickers spotted something in the river as they ate their lunch at Asham Wharf, a short way downstream from Rodmell. Letters of condolence from hundreds of Woolf's friends and admirers began to arrive at Monk's House.[37] Leonard dealt with the necessary inquest and arranged a cremation, which he attended alone. He buried the ashes in the garden at Monk's House, under one of the two elm trees they had named 'Leonard' and 'Virginia'. He and John Lehmann made the typescript of *Between the Acts* ready for publication, and Virginia Woolf's last novel came out in July.

It has gradually come to be recognized as one of her greatest books. It is restlessly, acrobatically experimental while at the same time taking its energy from all that is most traditional in English life: village talk, the old house, the landscape in the distance, the clatter of teacups, rhymes, songs, snatches of poetry, unpredictable summer weather. The pageant staged by Miss La Trobe has the same ambitious dynamics – pushing hard against the conventions even as it makes its fond, moving, comic tour through English history. Miss La Trobe worries all the way through about how it will be received. Will she make her audience feel anything? What is it all for? These are questions which reach back through Woolf's writing: to Rhoda in *The Waves*, knowing that she has something to give but wondering repeatedly, 'O, to whom?'; or Mr Ramsay on the terrace, agitated because his work will be forgotten; or Lily imagining her pictures rolled up in an attic; or Clarissa Dalloway thinking of her party: 'it was an offering; to combine; to create; but to whom?'[38]

Miss La Trobe disappears at the end of her pageant, refusing to acknowledge the applause. She doesn't want to be the centre of attention at the end; she wants to throw the focus back on the audience. Disoriented by this lack of an author to thank, the spectators in *Between the Acts* start getting uneasily to their feet, looking round at each other and making up their own minds about what they have seen.

Virginia Woolf at Tavistock Square, photographed by Gisèle Freund in June
1939. On the day of the sitting, Woolf was showing potential tenants around
the house, seeing Leonard's mother, making arrangements with T. S. Eliot
and May Sarton, and worrying about the chapter on Post-Impressionism
in her biography of Roger Fry. She had no desire to stop and sit still for
her portrait.

Afterwards

On the back of her last letter to Leonard, written just before she walked out to die, Woolf added a few practicalities: there were some of Roger's letters that he might need to find – they were in her desk. And, last of all, 'Will you destroy all my papers.'[1] It was a reasonable request, given the self-exposure of the diaries, the unguarded portraits of acquaintances, the unfinished memoirs, the journals and notebooks in which she sketched out her thoughts moment by moment. Literary bonfires included those of Thomas Hardy and Henry James.

The posthumous story of Virginia Woolf has been shaped by the fact that Leonard Woolf did not destroy her papers, but embarked instead on a project of editing and carefully timed publication which went on for the rest of his life. It was a way of keeping her memory alive. Every few years through the 1950s and 1960s Leonard made sure that there was a new book to refresh her image in her readers' minds. There were collections of her essays and, in 1954, a selection of extracts from her diaries. Understandably, Leonard thought the public had more business with Virginia's work than with any other part of her life, so his selection prioritized her exploration of her writing process, and he called it *A Writer's Diary*. It is the diary of a woman who lives for her work, who is acutely conscious of her states of mind, and whose daily life is made up of struggles with form, triumphs over language. Never before had a writing life

Vanessa Bell's cover design for *A Writer's Diary*. 'What sort of diary should I like mine to be?' Woolf asked herself in April 1919: 'Something loose knit, & yet not slovenly, so elastic that it will embrace any thing, solemn, slight or beautiful that comes into my mind.'

John Lehmann and Leonard Woolf reading Hogarth manuscripts, 1944.
On the top of the pile to the left of the lamp is a copy of *Between the Acts*,
published posthumously by the Hogarth Press in July 1941.

been so vividly and intimately narrated. The voice seemed very close, both formidable and familiar. Yes, we were there in the lonely study, and this was Virginia Woolf.

And then, later, another Woolf came in, laughing rather wildly, with a whole group of friends behind her. Between 1977 and 1984 the full diary appeared in five volumes, edited by Quentin Bell's wife Anne Olivier Bell. Now the writing life was mixed up with the social life and the family life and with jokes, holidays, errands, annoyances, campaigns. There was so much of it: every lunch party and shopping trip seemed to be here, every shade of changing emotion, a mass of contradictions, far more experience than seemed feasible for a single human life, and a short one at that. Anyone who reads the diaries will find it hard not to feel that *this* is Virginia Woolf.

But at the same time as the diaries there were (as Woolf said of Orlando) several thousand more selves emerging. Nigel Nicolson and his assistant Joanne Trautmann sat in the 'Virginia Room' at Sissinghurst Castle each summer through the mid-1970s and sorted through thousands of Woolf's letters. By 1980 there were six volumes of letters to place alongside the growing shelf of diaries. They revealed Woolf as one of the great letter-writers; and they revealed the character of her relationships with particular friends – especially when her side of a correspondence could be joined with its other half, as was the case for Lytton Strachey and Vita Sackville-West.[2]

The appearance of completeness has been one of the seductions for readers of Woolf, and one of the dangers. Feeling themselves to be in possession of all the evidence they need, commentators have often been bold in their judgments about very personal questions. Warier readers insert imaginary gaps where letters have not survived, or where weeks pass without a diary entry. We do not have Woolf's correspondence with her brother Adrian, for example; two of her closest friends,

E. M. Forster and Roger Fry, were certainly more central to her life than the scant letters suggest. When you live with someone you don't need to write to them, so we are not party to all those daily exchanges at Monk's House and Tavistock Square and never will be. Whatever else emerges from the depths of archives and desk drawers (like the early journal that turned up in 2002), there will be no finished picture of Virginia Woolf.[3]

Her biographers have been aware that they are offering an interpretation and not a final reckoning. The first was her nephew Quentin Bell, who was invited by Leonard to write an authorized biography. (That this was thirty years after Woolf's death suggests how anxious Leonard had been to wait for the right person and the right moment.) Bell's two-volume life, published in 1972, represented a sustained feat of sensitive judgment. Biographies by family members are not always known for their objectivity, but this one made candour a badge of honour, dealing openly with Woolf's illness, the question of abuse, the marriage, Vita, suicide. Bell's chronologically arranged narrative revealed very strikingly a pattern of alternating crisis and recovery. Almost every chapter brought a family death or a period of illness, but there was no lingering in the gloom. A resilient Woolf emerged from one thing after the next, full of new ideas for starting life afresh.

There were things that Bell purposely did not try to cover. He felt he should not set himself up as a literary critic, so the fine interplay between life and work was left to later interpreters. More controversially he did not see Woolf as a political thinker and left *Three Guineas* as a mistake best forgotten. This made the image of the mad aunt more discernible in Bell's account: she is repeatedly 'odd' in contrast to Leonard's practical commonsense. And this oddness in daily life is inseparable from her aesthetics. 'Her gift was for the pursuit of shadows, for the ghostly whispers of the mind and Pythian incomprehensibility', Bell wrote.[4] In reading her as a priestess of sensibility, he was making his sense of her limitations clear.

The fiercest opposition to this portrait came from feminist academics in America. Jane Marcus took *Three Guineas* and *The Years* as the central texts in her long campaign to reveal Woolf as an angry, highly politicized woman condemning a patriarchy that had kept her caged.[5] Inspired by Marcus, another academic, Louise DeSalvo, set out to show that every aspect of Woolf's life and work was shaped by her experience of abuse at the hands of the male inhabitants of Hyde Park Gate.[6] DeSalvo's book sold in its thousands in America and has been extremely influential, but for many readers it has been a source of frustration. Though she was studying one of the century's greatest intellects, DeSalvo chose a psychoanalytic method that privileged the work of the unconscious. In making Woolf so unrelentingly a victim and a sufferer, DeSalvo reinforced the existing image of fragility and in the process recast the novels as the products of a damaged mind.

Politicized, feminized, romanticized, sexualized, castigated, vindicated – the posthumous Virginia Woolf was the figurehead of opposing causes. She was a potent sign and symbol, even for people with no idea what she wrote. *Who's Afraid of Virginia Woolf?* Edward Albee's play had asked in 1962, using her name as shorthand for 'difficult' high culture. Was that what the author of *The Common Reader* stood for? The debates coalesced around questions of elitism and feminism. Was it alright for women to claim a heroine who refused to call herself a feminist? As issues of women's sexuality hit the headlines in the 1970s, Woolf's relationships came under scrutiny. Lyndall Gordon countered Marcus with a much more sympathetic account of the Woolf marriage in her fluid and imaginative 1984 biography, while opening a new controversy by downplaying the relationship with Vita.[7] What then of the lesbian icon? In the late twentieth century, Woolf's life became a battleground.[8]

All the more strange, then, that she was so often presented as being incapable of any battle at all. The melancholy, silent, white-laced Beresford portrait from 1902 was the one that people remembered: the one that was printed on posters and sent up in caricatures.[9] The idea of Woolf as a delicate aesthete was established early on in her life and persisted. When she wrote about Katherine Mansfield as 'A Terribly Sensitive Mind', she was partly getting even with a competitor, knowing she would be filed under that heading too. Some of the reports of her death implied that she was too fragile to cope with the war.

It is telling that when E. M. Forster paid tribute to Woolf in 1941, what he most wanted to do was to challenge that image. He pointed out how good she was at writing food. When the *boeuf en daube* comes in, says Forster, 'we peer down the shiny walls of the great casserole and get one of the best bits'.[10] He evoked a writer who was greedy, bodily, and sensuous. Speaking in the 1970s, Elizabeth Bowen remembered Woolf's huge vivacity. 'So I get a curious shock when I see people regarding her as a martyred [...] or definitely tragic sort of person, claimed by the darkness.'[11]

When Hermione Lee started work on a new authorized biography in 1991, she wanted to get away from the idea of Woolf as a mad genius and as the doomed victim of early abuse. She was interested in Woolf as a professional woman whose achievements came through extraordinary self-motivation and hard work. She was interested in what Woolf did, consciously, to get herself through periods of illness and to take control of her experiences. Lee's biography, when it came out in 1996, presented a woman of determination, self-knowledge, subtle eroticism, political insight, energy, good sense, and glittering

Virginia Woolf by Gisèle Freund in June 1939.

wit.[102] She was a confident 'subversive' in her life and her writing; she was the co-director of a successful publishing company; she was a partner in a long, loving marriage. Her physical presence and the material texture of her world became tangible, from the close rooms of Hyde Park Gate to the meetings of Rodmell Women's Institute. Lee's description of the General Strike was carefully filtered into her reading of the 'Time Passes' section of *To the Lighthouse* as an emphatic reminder of the outward engagement that shaped even the most apparently ethereal parts of Woolf's writing. There was no covering over Woolf's less appealing sides: yes, she was a snob, she was instinctively anti-Semitic, she could be extremely spiteful and jealous. But she had the nerve to acknowledge these things and to examine them. She knew her limitations and her fears (of egotism, madness, exposure) and made them one of her great fictional subjects. 'Virginia Woolf and Fear' was the title of one of Lee's university lectures in the late 1990s, but it ended as an affirmation of Woolf's courage, from which a new generation of readers could take heart.

Not surprisingly, Lee wondered why the Woolf of Stephen Daldry's 2002 film *The Hours*, played by Nicole Kidman with the famous addition of a prosthetic nose, had to be so very humourless and unworldly.[13] But the film as a whole, like the novel by Michael Cunningham on which it was based, is a gutsy revision of *Mrs Dalloway* with the acuity to take on Woolf at her sharpest. *The Hours* is a story about afterlives. It describes a series of people who have read *Mrs Dalloway* and whose lives, in their different ways, echo the patterns of experience traced in Woolf's novel. A young wife, trapped in a pristine suburban house in 1950s America, keeps up an immaculate smile for the benefit of her young son while trying to decide whether to kill herself; a dashing lesbian publisher in present-day New York hosts a party for a writer dying of AIDS, her fate linked with his as Clarissa is mysteriously linked with Septimus. It was apt that Cunningham chose for this novel the working title that Woolf used as she wrote *Mrs Dalloway*: it is as if Woolf's book is being opened up again, as if it is still being made.

This sense of an ongoing process was important too for Katie Mitchell, who directed a play based on *The Waves* in 2006.[14] Perhaps 'play' is not the right name, just as 'novel' seemed to Woolf a misleading word for some of her genre-shifting books. What Mitchell made was more a series of moments emerging from darkness, as actors filmed the tiny spotlit cameos they were constantly making and dismantling: a face in a mirror, a basin of water that suddenly seems like an ocean, bread rolls on a table laid sacramentally for a last supper. They were small works of art, with the qualities of a Chardin or a Hammershøi. Projected on to a screen above the stage, these images were immune from the clutter of props and cameras below. They came to feel like Woolf's 'moments of being', crystallizing one by one.

Like Katie Mitchell's white spotlight throwing details unexpectedly into relief, and as in Woolf's own idea of the biographer 'hanging up looking glasses at odd corners', contemporary critics keep bringing new facets of Woolf's life into view.[15] In the last few years there has been a book about her servants, and a biography of Leonard Woolf which asks that we see her from his point of view.[16] Olivia Laing has published a lyric account of a journey along the River Ouse, weaving the story of the Woolfs with the history of the landscape they loved.[17] The last volume of the superbly annotated six-volume edition of her collected essays appeared in 2011, making clear the range and volume of her critical writing as never before. Woolf's novels keep changing too. Our contemporary concerns teach us new ways of reading, so that some previously unnoticed image will suddenly stand out. And yet Woolf still arouses suspicion. Words like 'difficult', 'elitist', 'mad', 'unworldly' hover around her. East Sussex is not signposted 'Woolf Country' as Warwickshire is Shakespeare's country or Dorset is Hardy's. There is no Woolf theme park to match 'Dickens World' in Kent. Woolf's novels inspire experimental films rather than Sunday evening costume dramas.

Perhaps this will change as she comes to be more and more taught in schools and read for pleasure. But we'd better not settle down with her too comfortably. 'I'm the hare, a long way ahead of the hounds my critics', Woolf wrote as she taught herself not to mind what people said about *The Waves*.[18] It is a violent image, reminding us how violently she minded. But it is also an image of a writer's leaping confidence and agility, eluding capture, getting away. We are still in pursuit of Woolf, though we need not be like hounds. And seventy years after her death she is still a long way ahead, drawing us on. Like Daphne, the girl who runs like a hare in Ovid's *Metamorphoses*, Virginia Woolf has a habit of changing shape to stay alive.

Virginia Woolf reading, June 1926.

Notes

In the interests of consistency, references to the novels are to the Oxford World's Classics editions listed under 'Suggestions for Further Reading'. Letters are cited from the Hogarth Press six-volume edition, diaries are cited from the Penguin paperback five-volume edition, and essays from the Hogarth Press six-volume edition, except where otherwise stated. For full bibliographic information please see 'Suggestions for Further Reading'.

Foreword

1. VW to Violet Dickinson, 7 July 1907.
2. VW to Vanessa Bell [8? June 1911].
3. Ibid.
4. 'Modern Fiction' (1925) in *The Common Reader*, 146–54 (150), repr. in *Essays IV*, 157–65.
5. *Diary*, 23 February 1926.

1: Victorians 1882–1895

1. 'Old Bloomsbury' (*c.* 1922) in *Moments of Being*, 44.
2. Ibid., 45.
3. '22 Hyde Park Gate' (1921) in *Moments of Being*, 31.
4. As VW remembered the family friend Kitty Lushington having to do. '22 Hyde Park Gate', 32.
5. *Between the Acts*, 85: 'Just as she had brewed emotion; she spilt it.'
6. *The Waves*, 5.
7. 'Sketch of the Past' in *Moments of Being*, 94.
8. Woolf later wrote an introduction to a collection of Cameron's photographs: *Victorian Photographs of Famous Men and Fair Women* (1926; London: Chatto & Windus,

1996); Edward Burne-Jones, *The Annunciation*, 1876–9, Lady Lever Art Gallery, Liverpool.
9. 'Sketch of the Past' in *Moments of Being*, 94.
10. Ibid., 118.
11. *The Hyde Park Gate News*, ed. Gill Lowe (London: Hesperus, 2005).
12. Diane F. Gillespie in *The Sisters' Arts: The Writing and Painting of Virginia Woolf and Vanessa Bell* (Syracuse, NY: Syracuse Univ. Press, 1988) gives a fascinating account of their early certainty about this, and the evolving relationship between their work.
13. *Jacob's Room*, 75.
14. Leslie Stephen to Mrs Clifford, 25 July 1884, in Frederic William Maitland, *The Life and Letters of Leslie Stephen* (London: Duckworth, 1906), 384, and quoted in Hermione Lee, *Virginia Woolf* (London: Chatto & Windus, 1996), 29.
15. 'Sketch of the Past' in *Moments of Being*, 78.
16. *Jacob's Room*, 7.
17. *The Waves*, 12.

18. 'Sketch of the Past' in *Moments of Being*, 134.

19. *To the Lighthouse*, 105.

20. 'Sketch of the Past' in *Moments of Being*, 103.

21. *The Years*, 45.

22. 'Sketch of the Past' in *Moments of Being*, 102.

23. Ibid., 105.

2: Getting Through 1896–1904

1. Notes for 'Sketch of the Past', unpublished, quoted Lee, *Virginia Woolf*, 178.

2. Ibid.

3. Any retrospective diagnosis must be offered with extreme caution. On manic depression, see Thomas C. Caramagno, *The Flight of the Mind: Virginia Woolf's Art and Manic-Depressive Illness* (Berkeley, CA: Univ. of California Press, 1992). Lee, *Virginia Woolf*, 175–200, comprehensively lays out the evidence for Woolf's medical history and weighs alternative interpretations, concluding that we cannot be sure what caused VW's mental illness: 'We can only look at what it did to her, and what she did with it' (199).

4. 1897 Journal in *Passionate Apprentice*, 26.

5. Ibid., 90.

6. Ibid., 114.

7. Ibid., 134.

8. Ibid., 132.

9. *Diary*, 15 February 1937.

10. Ibid., 1 May 1934.

11. 'Sketch of the Past' in *Moments of Being*, 82.

12. Louise DeSalvo claims in *Virginia Woolf: The Impact of Childhood Sexual Abuse on Her Life and Work* (London: The Women's Press, 1989) that 'virtually every male member' of the 'pathologically dysfunctional' Stephen/Duckworth family was involved in child abuse (2). Such a reading depends on wilful exaggeration and guesswork, as does DeSalvo's assertion of a 'causal connection' (109) between this childhood abuse and Woolf's illness. Caramagno, in *Flight of the Mind*, responded by emphasizing the biochemical causes and effects of manic depression.

13. 'Reminiscences' (1908) in *Moments of Being*, 29.

14. '22 Hyde Park Gate' (1921), ibid., 42.

15. E.g. 'Thoughts on Social Success' (1903) in *Passionate Apprentice*, 167.

16. Ibid., 168.

17. *Mrs Dalloway*, 145.

18. 'Sketch of the Past' in *Moments of Being*, 140.

19. Warboys Journal (1899) in *Passionate Apprentice*, 145.

20. VW to Thoby Stephen, 5 November [1901].

21. See, e.g. 'Rambling round Evelyn', in *The Common Reader*, 78–85; repr. in *Essays IV*, 91–8.

22. 'Retrospect' (1903) in *Passionate Apprentice*, 187.

23. VW to Violet Dickinson [September 1902].

24. Published as *Sir Leslie Stephen's Mausoleum Book*, ed. Alan Bell (Oxford: Clarendon Press, 1977).

25. *Diary*, 28 November 1928.

26. Frederic William Maitland, *The Life and Letters of Leslie Stephen* (London: Duckworth, 1906), 474–7; VW's contribution repr. in *Essays I*, 127–30.

27. VW to Madge Vaughan [mid-December 1904].

28. VW to Lady Robert Cecil, 22 December 1904.

29. 1904–5 Journal in *Passionate Apprentice*, 216.

30. VW to Violet Dickinson [early January 1905]. The payment was for two reviews and an essay, 'Literary Geography', about a visit to the Brontë parsonage at Haworth.

31. Leslie Stephen to Charles Eliot Norton, 11 March 1883, Maitland, *Life and Letters*, 337.

32. 1905 Journal in *Passionate Apprentice*, 219.

3: Setting Up 1905–1915

1. 'Old Bloomsbury' in *Moments of Being*, 46.

2. VW to Violet Dickinson, 1 October 1905.

3. VW to Violet Dickinson, 16 January 1906.

4. Cornwall Journal (1905) in *Passionate Apprentice*, 290.

5. Cornwall Journal (1905), ibid., 294.

6. 1904–5 Journal, ibid., 276–7.

7. 'Greece 1906', ibid., 333.

8. VW to Violet Dickinson, 23 December 1906.

9. VW to Violet Dickinson, 22 September 1907.

10. VW to Vanessa Bell [October? 1907].

11. VW to Vanessa Bell, 29 August 1908.

12. VW to Clive Bell, 28 August 1908.

13. VW to Vanessa Bell, 25 December 1909.

14. 'Lady Hester Stanhope' (1910) in *Essays I*, 325.

15. VW to Clive Bell, 26 December 1909.

16. VW to Vanessa Bell, 24 June 1910.

17. VW to Vanessa Bell, 28 July 1910.

18. Vanessa Bell, 'Notes on Bloomsbury' (1951) in *The Bloomsbury Group: A Collection of Memoirs*, ed. S. P. Rosenbaum (London: Taylor & Francis, 1975), 81.

19. VW to Violet Dickinson, 27 November 1910.

20. VW to Molly MacCarthy [March 1911].

21. *The Waves*, 44, 171.

22. VW to Violet Dickinson [June? 1906].

23. VW to Vanessa Bell, 10 August 1908.

24. VW to Ottoline Morrell, 9 November 1911.

25. VW to Leonard Woolf, 2 December 1911.

26. VW to Violet Dickinson, 4 June 1912.

27. Leonard Woolf, *Beginning Again: An Autobiography of the Years 1911–1918* (London: Hogarth Press, 1964), 57.

28. VW to Leonard Woolf, 1 May 1912.

29. VW to Janet Case, June 1912.

30. VW to Lady Robert Cecil, June 1912.

31. VW to Violet Dickinson, 1 January 1911. An earlier version of the novel has been pieced together from drafts and published as *Melymbrosia*, ed. Louise DeSalvo (1982; Berkeley, CA: Cleis Press, 2002).

32. *The Voyage Out*, 245.

33. Ibid., 161.

34. Ibid., 337.

35. Ibid., 341.

36. VW to Leonard Woolf, 4 December 1913.

4: Making a Mark 1916–1922

1. VW to Katherine Cox, 12 February 1916.

2. VW to Ethel Smyth, 16 October 1930.

3. *Night and Day*, 149.

4. Ibid., 530.

5. *Diary*, 2 January 1923.

6. VW to Violet Dickinson, 10 April 1917; VW to Lady Robert Cecil, 14 April 1917.

7. 'A Mark on the Wall' (1917) was published with Leonard's story 'Three Jews' as *Two Stories*, the first publication by the Hogarth Press. Reprinted in *The Mark on the Wall and Other Short Fiction*, ed. David Bradshaw (Oxford: Oxford Univ. Press, 2001), 3–10.

8. 'An Unwritten Novel' (1920), repr. ibid., 18–29.

9. *Diary*, 25 October 1920.

10. Ibid., 20 January 1919.

11. Ibid., 15 February 1919.

12. Ibid., 22 August 1922.

13. VW to Katherine Arnold-Forster, 12 August 1919.

14. *Diary*, 15 September 1921.

15. VW to Vanessa Bell, 28 June 1916.

16. *Diary*, 22 November 1917.

17. Ibid., 2 November 1917.

18. VW to Violet Dickinson, 27 November 1919.

19. *Diary*, 22 March 1921, quoting Psalm 126.

20. Ibid., 18 May 1919.

21. VW to Lytton Strachey, 12 October 1918.

22. *Diary*, 13 February 1920.

23. Ibid., 8 April 1921.

24. Katherine Mansfield to Virginia Woolf, 24? June 1917, *Katherine Mansfield: Selected Letters*, ed. Vincent O'Sullivan (Oxford: Clarendon Press, 1989), 56.

25. *Diary*, 25 August 1920. Angela Smith in *Katherine Mansfield and Virginia Woolf: A Public of Two* (Oxford: Oxford Univ. Press, 1999), writes of an 'uncanny doubling' in their writing. Hermione Lee in *Virginia Woolf*, 386–401, reads the relationship with Mansfield as one of the most important, complicated and haunting of Woolf's life.

26. Ibid., 13 March 1921.
27. Ibid., 22 March 1921.
28. Ibid., 23 June 1922.
29. VW to Roger Fry, 6 May 1922.
30. *Diary*, 16 August 1922.
31. Ibid., 26 September 1920.
32. In response to Arnold Bennett's *Our Women. Diary*, 26 September 1920.
33. VW to E. M. Forster, 21 January 1922.
34. *Jacob's Room*, 4.
35. Ibid., 36.
36. Ibid., 48.
37. Ibid., 149.
38. Ibid., 245.
39. *Diary*, 13 November 1922.

5: 'Drawn on and on' 1923–1925

1. VW to Gerald Brenan, 25 December 1922.
2. *Diary*, 29 October 1922.
3. *Mrs Dalloway*, 4.
4. *Diary*, 8 October 1922.
5. Ibid., 15 October 1923.
6. Ibid., 15 October 1923.
7. VW to Gerald Brenan, 13 May 1923.
8. VW to Marjorie Joad, 15 February 1925.
9. VW to Gwen Raverat, 1 May 1925.
10. VW to Vanessa Bell, 27 April 1924.
11. *Mrs Dalloway*, 3.
12. *Diary*, 5 September 1925; *Diary*, 17 February 1926.
13. Ibid., 15 September 1924.
14. VW to Vita Sackville-West, 15 September 1924.

15. VW to Jacques Raverat, 26 December 1924.
16. VW to Jacques Raverat, 24 January 1925.
17. *Diary*, 15 September 1924.
18. *The Common Reader*, 106–33 and repr. in *Essays IV*, 118–45: 'Taylors and Edgeworths', 'Laetitia Pilkington', 'Miss Ormerod'. Thanks to Woolf and much subsequent scholarship on nineteenth-century women's lives, Woolf's subjects are much less obscure today.
19. *To the Lighthouse*, 42.
20. *Diary*, 7 January 1923.
21. Ibid., 16 January 1923.
22. Ibid., 5 May 1924.
23. Ibid., 21 June 1924.
24. Ibid., 15 October 1923.
25. *Mrs Dalloway*, 165.
26. VW to Gwen Raverat, 8 April 1925.

6: 'This is it' 1925–1927

1. Manuscript notebook quoted in Lee, *Virginia Woolf*, 475.
2. 'Sketch of the Past' in *Moments of Being*, 93.
3. *Diary*, 28 November 1928.
4. Vanessa Bell to VW, 11 May 1927 in *Letters* 3, 572 (appendix).
5. VW to Vita Sackville-West, 21 February 1927.
6. *Diary*, 2 August 1926.
7. Ibid., 14 June 1925.
8. *To the Lighthouse*, 170.
9. Ibid., 165.
10. *Mrs Dalloway*, 165.
11. *To the Lighthouse*, 170.

12. *Diary*, 27 February 1926.
13. Ibid.
14. *To the Lighthouse*, 169.
15. 'Sketch of the Past' in *Moments of Being* 85.

7: A Writer's Holiday 1927–1928

1. In her 1960 preface to *Orlando*, repr. in *The Mulberry Tree*, ed. Hermione Lee (1986; London: Vintage, 1999), 131–2.
2. *Diary*, 14 March 1927.
3. Ibid., 20 September 1927.
4. Ibid., 18 March 1928.
5. *To the Lighthouse*, 10.
6. *Diary*, 14 March 1927.
7. VW to Vita Sackville-West, 15 March 1927.
8. *Diary*, 20 December 1927.
9. *Orlando*, 82–91.
10. *Diary*, 21 December 1925; *Diary*, 23 February 1926.
11. VW to Vita Sackville-West, 5 February 1927.
12. Vita Sackville-West to Harold Nicolson, 17 August 1926, in *Vita and Harold: The Letters of Vita Sackville-West and Harold Nicolson*, ed. Nigel Nicolson (East Rutherford, NJ: Putnam, 1992), 159.
13. VW to Vita Sackville-West, 23 March 1927.
14. *Orlando*, 114.
15. See Vita Sackville-West's family history *Pepita* (London: Hogarth Press, 1937).
16. VW to Gerald Brenan,

1 December 1923.
17. *A Room of One's Own*, 104.
18. *Diary*, 20 September 1927.

8: Voices 1929–1932

1. *The Waves*, 234.
2. Vanessa Bell to VW, 3 May 1927 in *Selected Letters of Vanessa Bell*, ed. Regina Marler (London: Bloomsbury, 1993).
3. *Diary*, 23 June 1929.
4. VW to G. L. Dickinson, 27 October 1931.
5. *The Waves*, 176; see. *Diary* 16 February 1932, 'by way of proving my credentials'.
6. *Mrs Dalloway*, 7.
7. VW to Ethel Smyth, 28 August 1930.
8. Nigel Nicolson in *Recollections of Virginia Woolf*, ed. Joan Russell Noble (1972; Harmondsworth: Penguin, 1975), 156.
9. *Diary*, 26 December 1929.
10. Ibid., 25 September 1929.
11. Ibid., 26 January 1930.
12. Ibid., 7 November 1928.
13. Ibid., 28 March 1930.
14. Ibid., 9 April 1930.
15. VW to Violet Dickinson, 7 July 1907.
16. *Diary*, 7 January 1931.
17. Ibid., 16 September 1929.
18. Ibid., 16 February 1930; ibid., 8 September 1930.
19. Ibid., 7 February 1931.
20. Ibid., 21 February 1930.
21. VW to Ethel Smyth, 27 February 1930.

22. *Diary*, 21 February 1930.

23. VW to Ethel Smyth, 18 June 1932.

24. VW to Vita Sackville-West, 4 August 1931.

25. *Diary*, 20 August 1930.

26. VW to Vita Sackville-West, 6 November 1930.

27. VW to Ethel Smyth, 15 August 1930.

28. 'The Novels of Thomas Hardy', in *The Common Reader II*, 245–57 (246), repr. in *Essays IV*, 561–71.

29. Ibid., 250.

30. VW to Ethel Smyth, 29 December 1931.

31. VW to Hugh Walpole, 16 July 1930.

32. VW to Ethel Smyth, 2 August 1930.

33. VW to the editor of the *New Statesman*, 28 October 1933.

9: The Argument of Art 1932–1938

1. *Diary*, 25 April 1933.

2. Ibid.

3. Ibid., 13 September 1935: 'The difficulty is always at the beginning of chapters or sections where a whole new mood has to be caught plumb in the centre.'

4. Ibid., 31 May 1933. Woolf's draft of this 'novel-essay' has been published and offers a glimpse of Woolf at work in the 1930s. See *The Pargiters*, ed. Mitchell A. Leaska (New York, NY: New York Public Library, 1977).

5. See *Diary*, 16 August 1933 and her essay 'The Novels of Turgenev' (1933), repr. in *Essays VI*, 8–17: 'few combine the fact and the vision, and the rare quality that we find in Turgenev is the result of this double process' (11).

6. *Diary*, 19 December 1932.

7. Ibid., 2 November 1932.

8. For a helpful and nuanced discussion, see Maren Linett, 'The Jew in the Bath', *Modern Fiction Studies* 48:2 (2002), 341–61. On prejudice and offensiveness more generally, see Hermione Lee, 'Virginia Woolf and Offence', in *The Art of Literary Biography*, ed. John Batchelor (Oxford: Oxford Univ. Press, 1994).

9. For a detailed account, see Alison Light, *Mrs Woolf and the Servants* (London: Fig Tree, 2007).

10. *Diary*, 2 September 1934.

11. Ibid., 12 September 1934.

12. VW to Ethel Smyth, 11 September 1934.

13. *Diary*, 19 January 1935.

14. Ibid., 29 October 1933.

15. Ibid., 17 July 1935.

16. Ibid., 15 October 1935.

17. Ibid., 29 December 1935.

18. Ibid., 3 January 1936.

19. Ibid., 5 November 1936.

20. Ibid., 30 November 1936.

21. Ibid., 29 December 1935.

22. *The Years*, 389, 401.

23. Ibid., 351.

24. Ibid., 413.

25. *Diary*, 15 May 1940.

26. VW to Julian Bell, 28 June 1936.

27. *Diary*, 12 October 1937.

28. Ibid., 22 October 1937.
29. Ibid., 12 October 1937.
30. *The Years*, 371.

10: Sussex 1938–1941

1. *Diary*, 13 September 1938.
2. Ibid., 14 September 1938.
3. VW to Ethel Smyth, 29 August 1938.
4. *Diary*, 22 June 1940.
5. Ibid., 25 July 1940.
6. Ibid., 29 June 1939, 11 December 1938, 23 June 1939.
7. *Roger Fry*, 150, 161.
8. Ibid., 104.
9. Ibid., 202.
10. *Diary*, 28 August 1939.
11. Ibid., 3 September 1922.
12. *Between the Acts*, 5, 62.
13. *Diary*, 9 June 1940.
14. *Between the Acts*, 107.
15. Ibid., 114–15.
16. *Diary*, 12 July 1940.
17. Ibid., 16 August 1940.
18. Ibid., 20 October 1940.
19. Ibid.
20. Ibid., 28 August 1940.
21. Ibid., 22 June 1940.
22. 'Sketch of the Past' in *Moments of Being*, 108.
23. Ibid., 116.
24. Ibid., 146–7.
25. Ibid., 159.
26. Ibid., 154.
27. *Between the Acts*, 189.
28. *Diary*, 14 October 1938.
29. The notes and drafts are published with extensive commentary as '"Anon" and "The Reader": Virginia Woolf's Last Essays', ed. Brenda Silver, *Twentieth Century Literature*, 25 (1979), 356–441 and repr. *Essays VI*, 580–607.
30. *Diary*, 24 December 1940.
31. Hermione Lee identifies 'egotism' as 'one of Woolf's most important words': see *Virginia Woolf*, 5–7, 17–18, 72, and on its opposite, anonymity, 745–67.
32. 'Sketch of the Past' in *Moments of Being*, 149.
33. VW to Ethel Smyth, 1 February 1941.
34. *Diary*, 26 January 1941.
35. VW to Leonard Woolf [28 March 1941].
36. VW to Vanessa Bell [23? March 1941].
37. These letters, many of them eloquent and moving tributes to VW, are published as *Afterwords: Letters on the Death of Virginia Woolf*, ed. Sybil Oldfield (Edinburgh: Edinburgh Univ. Press, 2005).
38. *The Waves*, 44; *Mrs Dalloway*, 103 (also 20, 50, 57).

Afterwards

1. VW to Leonard Woolf [28 March 1941].
2. *Virginia Woolf and Lytton Strachey: Letters*, ed. James Strachey and Leonard Woolf (London: Chatto & Windus, 1956); *The Letters of Vita Sackville-West to Virginia Woolf*, ed. Louise DeSalvo and Mitchell A. Leaska (London: Hutchinson, 1984).

3. *Carlyle's House and Other Sketches*, ed. David Bradshaw (London: Hesperus, 2003). This journal dates from 1909. It seems probable that VW kept other journals in the immediate pre-war period; something more may come to light.

4. Quentin Bell, *Virginia Woolf* (London: Hogarth Press, 1972), 186.

5. Jane Marcus, *Virginia Woolf and the Languages of Patriarchy* (Bloomington, IN: Indiana Univ. Press, 1987).

6. DeSalvo, *Virginia Woolf: The Impact of Childhood Sexual Abuse on Her Life and Work*.

7. Lyndall Gordon, *Virginia Woolf: A Writer's Life* (Oxford: Oxford Univ. Press, 1984).

8. The story of Woolf's posthumous reputation is told by Regina Marler in *Bloomsbury Pie* (London: Virago, 1998).

9. On the iconography of the Beresford photographs, see Lee, *Virginia Woolf*, 246, and Brenda Silver, *Virginia Woolf: Icon* (Chicago, IL: Chicago Univ. Press, 1999), 130.

10. *Recollections of Virginia Woolf*, 237.

11. Ibid., 62.

12. Hermione Lee, *Virginia Woolf* (London: Chatto & Windus, 2006).

13. See Hermione Lee, 'Virginia Woolf's Nose', in *Body Parts: Essays on Life Writing* (London: Chatto & Windus, 2005), 28–44.

14. *Waves*, dir. Katie Mitchell, premiered at the National Theatre, London, 18 November 2006.

15. 'The Art of Biography' (1939) in *Essays VI*, 186.

16. Light, *Virginia Woolf and the Servants*; Victoria Glendinning, *Leonard Woolf* (London: Simon & Schuster, 2006).

17. Olivia Laing, *To the River: A Journey beneath the Surface* (Edinburgh: Canongate, 2011).

18. *Diary*, 22 September 1931.

Suggestions for Further Reading

Works by Virginia Woolf (in order of first publication and in the editions used). Drafts of almost all the novels are now available in published form and offer extraordinarily rich insights into Woolf's processes of writing and revision.

Virginia Woolf, *The Voyage Out* (1915), ed. Lorna Sage. Oxford: Oxford Univ. Press, 2001.

—— *Night and Day* (1919), ed. Suzanne Raitt. Oxford: Oxford Univ. Press, 1992.

—— *Jacob's Room* (1922), ed. Kate Flint. Oxford: Oxford Univ. Press, 2005.

—— *The Common Reader* (1925). London: Vintage, 2003.

—— *Mrs Dalloway* (1925), ed. David Bradshaw. Oxford: Oxford Univ. Press, 2008.

—— *To the Lighthouse* (1927), ed. David Bradshaw. Oxford: Oxford Univ. Press, 2006.

—— *Orlando: A Biography* (1928), ed. Rachel Bowlby. Oxford: Oxford Univ. Press, 1992.

—— *A Room of One's Own* (1928) and *Three Guineas* (1938), ed. Morag Shiach. Oxford: Oxford Univ. Press, 1998.

—— *The Waves* (1931), ed. Gillian Beer. Oxford: Oxford Univ. Press, 1992.

—— *The Common Reader II* (1932). London: Vintage, 2003.

—— *Flush* (1933), ed. Kate Flint. Oxford: Oxford Univ. Press, 1998.

—— *The Years* (1937), ed. Hermione Lee. Oxford: Oxford Univ. Press, 1992.

—— *Roger Fry: A Biography* (1940). London: Vintage, 2003.

—— *Between the Acts* (1941), ed. Frank Kermode. Oxford: Oxford Univ. Press, 1992.

—— *The Letters of Virginia Woolf,* ed. Nigel Nicolson, assisted by Joanne Trautmann Banks. 6 vols. London: Hogarth Press, 1975–80.

—— *Moments of Being,* ed. Jeanne Schulkind. 1976. Revised by Hermione Lee. London: Pimlico, 2002.

—— '"Anon" and "The Reader": Virginia Woolf's Last Essays', ed. Brenda Silver, *Twentieth Century Literature,* 25 (1979), 356–441.

—— *The Diary of Virginia Woolf,* ed. Anne Olivier Bell, assisted by Andrew McNeillie. 5 vols (1977–84). Harmondsworth: Penguin, 1979–85.

—— *The Essays of Virginia Woolf.* Vols 1–3 ed. Andrew McNeillie, Vols 4–6 ed. Stuart N. Clarke. London: Hogarth Press, 1986–2011.

—— *A Passionate Apprentice: The Early Journals of Virginia Woolf*, ed. Mitchell A. Leaska. London: Hogarth Press, 1990.

—— *The Mark on the Wall and Other Short Fiction*, ed. David Bradshaw. Oxford: Oxford Univ. Press, 2001.

—— with Vanessa and Thoby Stephen, *The Hyde Park Gate News*, ed. Gill Lowe. London: Hesperus Press, 2005.

Biography

The standard biography is *Virginia Woolf* by Hermione Lee (London: Chatto & Windus, 1996). Quentin Bell's biography of his aunt (London: Hogarth Press, 1972) still has much to offer, as does *Virginia Woolf: A Writer's Life* by Lyndall Gordon (Oxford: Oxford Univ. Press, 1984). John Mepham's *Virginia Woolf: A Literary Life* (London: Macmillan, 1991) gives clear and helpful readings of the work in a biographical context. Because so many of Woolf's friends were writers, there are abundant first-hand accounts of her. Some of these are gathered in *Recollections of Virginia Woolf*, ed. Joan Russell Noble (1972; Harmondsworth: Penguin, 1975), which can still give the frisson of immediacy.

Books By and About Woolf's Family and Friends

Sir Leslie Stephen's Mausoleum Book (Oxford: Clarendon Press, 1977) is a remarkable document of Victorian mourning and gives some insight into the mood of Hyde Park Gate after 1895. Leonard Woolf's autobiography (5 vols; London: Hogarth Press, 1960–9) is one of the major sources for understanding the Woolfs, their daily lives and commitments, and particularly the work of the Hogarth Press. Roger Fry's ideas about aesthetics were one of the great influences on Woolf, and a reading of his essays in *Vision & Design* (1920; Mineola, NY: Dover, 1981) will send one back to Woolf's novels newly alert to their formal qualities.

Among the biographies of Woolf's friends, see especially Michael Holroyd's life of Lytton Strachey and Frances Spalding's biographies of Roger Fry, Vanessa Bell, and Duncan Grant. Victoria Glendinning has written lives of Vita Sackville-West and, most recently, Leonard Woolf.

Critical Studies of Woolf's Work

Of all the hundreds of books on Woolf's work, here are ten good places to start:

Rachel Bowlby, *Virginia Woolf: Feminist Destinations*. Oxford: Blackwell, 1988.

Gillian Beer, *Virginia Woolf: The Common Ground*. Edinburgh: Edinburgh Univ. Press, 1996.

Julia Briggs, *Reading Virginia Woolf.*
Edinburgh: Edinburgh Univ.
Press, 2006.

Maria DiBattista, *Virginia Woolf's
Major Novels.* New Haven: Yale
Univ. Press, 1980.

Jane de Gay, *Virginia Woolf's Novels
and the Literary Past.* Edinburgh:
Edinburgh Univ. Press, 2006.

Jane Goldman, *The Cambridge
Introduction to Virginia Woolf.*
Cambridge: Cambridge Univ.
Press, 2006.

Hermione Lee, *The Novels of
Virginia Woolf.* 1977. London:
Routledge, 2010.

Laura Marcus, *Writers and their
Work: Virginia Woolf.* Tonbridge:
Northcote, 1997, revised 2004.

Allen McLaurin, *Virginia Woolf:
The Echoes Enslaved.* Cambridge:
Cambridge Univ. Press, 1973.

Susan Sellers, ed. *The Cambridge
Companion to Virginia Woolf.*
Cambridge: Cambridge Univ.
Press, 2000, revised 2010.

Virginia Woolf on Film

Orlando, 1992, dir. Sally Potter,
with Tilda Swinton as Orlando.

Mrs Dalloway, 1997, dir. Marleen
Gorris, with Vanessa Redgrave
as Clarissa.

The Hours, 2002, dir. Stephen
Daldry, adapted from the novel
by Michael Cunningham, with
Nicole Kidman as Virginia Woolf.

Excursions

Quentin Bell was right to envisage
(in a comic family play in 1936)
that Charleston a century later
would be full of tourists examining
the furniture. The house and
garden are open from April to
October, with an annual literary
festival in May and temporary
exhibitions in the gallery.
See www.charleston.org.uk.

Monk's House, Rodmell, East
Sussex, is owned by the National
Trust and open two afternoons a
week April to October.
See www.nationaltrust.org.uk.

Asheham was bought in 1932 by
the cement company which was
already quarrying the surrounding
land. For many years it stood
derelict, and was eventually
demolished in 1994.

None of Woolf's London houses is
open to visitors, but 22 Hyde Park
Gate is largely unchanged on the
outside, as is Hogarth House in
Richmond. Fifty-two Tavistock
Square was demolished after the
bomb damage.

The 'Virginia Woolf Society
of Great Britain' (www.
virginiawoolfsociety.co.uk)
arranges regular meetings,
readings, and visits, and publishes
the quarterly *Virginia Woolf
Bulletin*. For readers in America
and the rest of the world there is
the 'International Virginia Woolf
Society': www.utoronto.ca/IVWS

Credits

Illustrations

All images by Vanessa Bell are © Estate of Vanessa Bell, courtesy
Henrietta Garnett

Frontispiece Estate of Gisèle Freund/IMEC Images; **10** Photo George
Beresford. National Portrait Gallery, London; **15** Private Collection/
Bridgeman Art Library; **17** G.F. Watts, *Portrait of Sir Leslie Stephen*, 1878.
National Portrait Gallery, London; **22** Private Collection; **27** Private
Collection/Bridgeman Art Library; **34, 37** Estate of Professor Quentin Bell
by permission of Julian Bell; **40** Vanessa Bell, *The Bedroom, Gordon Square*,
1912. Photo Anthony d'Offay Gallery; **48** Photograph by Vanessa Bell;
51 Dora Carrington, *Asheham House*; **53** © Estate of Vanessa Bell, courtesy
Henrietta Garnett; **60** Tate Archives, London; **62** Vanessa Bell, *Clive Bell
and Family*, Leicester Museum; **67** Getty Images; **68** Mark Gertler, *The Pond
at Garsington*, 1916, Leeds Art Galleries; **71** Photo Ramsey & Muspratt,
Cambridge; **74** Roger Fry, *E.M. Forster*, Private Collection; **77** Vanessa Bell,
A Conversation, 1913–16. Courtauld Institute Gallery, London; **82** Vanessa
Bell, *Autumn Announcements*, 1924, for Hogarth Press; **86** Sasha/Getty
Images; **87** Maurice Beck/Vogue; **89** Vanessa Bell jacket design for *Mrs
Dalloway* by Virginia Woolf, c.1925. Photo Eileen Tweedy; **92** Photograph
by Julia Margaret Cameron; **94** Vanessa Bell, *Leonard Woolf*, 1925. National
Portrait Gallery, London; **97** Private Collection/Bridgeman Art Library;
101 Vita Sackville West from *Orlando, A Biography*, by Virginia Woolf,
London 1928; **102** Vanessa Bell, endpapers for *Flush* by Virginia Woolf,
London 1933; **105** Dora Carrington. *Lytton Strachey;* **108** Roger Fry, *View
of Cassis*, 1925. Musée d'Art Moderne, Paris; **110** Photo Edwin Smith;
115 Ramsey & Muspratt, Cambridge; **117** Vanessa Bell, jacket design for *The
Waves* by Virginia Woolf, London 1931; **121** Estate of Professor Quentin
Bell by permission of Julian Bell; **130** Roger Fry, jacket design for *Cezanne, A
Study of His Development* by Roger Fry, London, 1927; **133** Fox Photos/
Getty Images; **137** Private Collection; **139** Vanessa Bell, *Roger Fry and Julian*

Bell at Charleston. King's College, Cambridge; **145** Photo Edwin Smith; **149** Diana Gardner, *The Hedge Hoppers,* 1940. © Estate of Diana Gardner. Illustration by permission of Cecil Woof Publishers, London; **156, 159** Estate of Gisèle Freund/IMEC Images; **161** Vanessa Bell, drawing for jacket of *A Writer's Diary,* edited by Leonard Woolf, London 1953. Photo Eileen Tweedy; **162** Hulton Deutsch/Corbis; **167** Estate of Gisèle Freund/IMEC Images; **171** Lady Ottoline Morrell, *Virginia Woolf (née Stephen),* 1926. National Portrait Gallery, London.

Text extracts

I am extremely grateful to the Society of Authors, on behalf of the Estate of Virginia Woolf, for allowing me to quote from Woolf's fiction.

Excerpts from *The Letters of Virginia Woolf,* edited by Nigel Nicolson and Joanne Trautmann, published by The Hogarth Press. Reprinted by permission of The Random House Group Ltd.

Excerpts from *The Diary of Virginia Woolf,* edited by Anne Olivier Bell, published by The Hogarth Press. Reprinted by permission of The Random House Group Ltd.

Excerpts from *Moments of Being* by Virginia Woolf, published by Chatto & Windus. Reprinted by permission of the Random House Group Ltd.

Excerpts from *The Essays of Virginia Woolf,* Volume IV, 1925–28, Text by Virginia Woolf copyright © Quentin Bell and Angelica Garnett 1925, 1926, 1927, 1928, 1994, introduction and editorial notes copyright © Andrew McNeillie 1994, reprinted by permission of the Random House Group Ltd.

Excerpts from *A Passionate Apprentice: The Early Journals of Virginia Woolf,* copyright © 1990 by Quentin Bell and Angelica Garnett, reprinted by permission of the Random House Group Ltd

Index

Page numbers in *italics* refer to illustrations and captions

Also by Alexandra Harris

Romantic Moderns
English Writers, Artists and the Imagination
from Virginia Woolf to John Piper

Winner of the *Guardian* First Book Award

'A joy to read' *Sunday Times*

'It would be impossible to over-emphasise what a clever
book *Romantic Moderns* is … not just an important book
but a deeply pleasurable one, too' *Guardian*

'Teems with fascinating detail …Well researched, wide-ranging
and generously illustrated, the book contains many
delights and surprises' *Daily Telegraph*

'Brilliant, delightfully readable … thoroughly invigorating'
Financial Times

'Remarkable … Harris's insights are based on a close, imaginative
reading of collaborations and connections mapped through
friendships and unlikely encounters. Her book is full of vivid
snapshots, telling detail and beguiling loose ends'
Times Literary Supplement

Weatherland
Writers and Artists Under English Skies

A Book of the Year in *The Times, Sunday Times, Observer,
Independent* and *Times Literary Supplement*

'Gathers all the written English centuries and sets them
dancing to the seasons on the head of its pin'
Ali Smith, *Times Literary Supplement*

'A dazzling journey through the weather-worlds
of English culture and history' *Robert Macfarlane*

'A brilliant, beautiful and sensual book' *Sunday Times*

' Splendid … its glory is in the detail, in its recording of
facts and lives, atmospheres and words, quirks of feeling
and behaviour' A. S. Byatt, *Guardian*

'A fascinating portrait of that most British
of preoccupations' *Independent*